DEPARTMENT OF FAR EASTERN HISTORY,
AUSTRALIAN NATIONAL UNIVERSITY
AND
ASIAN STUDIES ASSOCIATION OF AUSTRALIA

East Asia Series

POPULIST NATIONALISM IN PREWAR JAPAN
A BIOGRAPHY OF NAKANO SEIGŌ

DEPARTMENT OF FAR EASTERN HISTORY, ANU
AND
ASIAN STUDIES ASSOCIATION OF AUSTRALIA

East Asia Series

Leslie Russell Oates, *Populist Nationalism in Prewar Japan: A Biography of Nakano Seigō*
Paul Rule, *K'ung-tzu or Confucius? The Jesuit Interpretation of Confucianism*
Beverley Hooper, *The Elimination of the Western Presence in China; The Communist Victory and its Aftermath*

EDITORIAL COMMITTEE

Wang Gungwu (Chairman)	Australian National University
Jennifer Cushman (Secretary)	Australian National University
Andrew Fraser	Australian National University
J.S. Gregory	La Trobe University
Stephen Large	Flinders University

Populist Nationalism in Prewar Japan
A biography of Nakano Seigō

Leslie Russell Oates

George Allen & Unwin
Sydney London Boston

© Leslie Russell Oates 1985
This book is copyright under the Berne Convention.
No reproduction without permission.

First published in 1985 by
George Allen & Unwin Australia Pty Ltd
8 Napier Street, North Sydney, NSW 2060 Australia
in association with
Department of Far Eastern History,
Australian National University
and
Asian Studies Association of Australia

George Allen & Unwin (Publishers) Ltd
18 Park Lane, Hemel Hempstead, Herts HP2 4TE England

Allen & Unwin Inc.
Fifty Cross Street, Winchester, Mass 01890 USA

Oates, L. R. (Leslie Russell), 1925–
    Populist nationalism in prewar Japan:
    a biography of Nakano Seigō.

    Bibliography.
    ISBN 0 86861 111 5.

    1. Nakano Seigō, 1886–1943. 2. Statesman—Japan—
    Biography. 3. Japan—Politics and government—1926–
    I. Australian National University. Dept. of Far Eastern History.
    II. Asian Studies Association of Australia. III. Title.

952. 03'3' 0924

Library of Congress Catalog Card Number: 84-71887

Set in 10/11pt Times by Asco Trade Typesetting Ltd, Hong Kong
Printed in Hong Kong

Contents

Preface	vi
Introduction	vii
1 Launched on a world of expanding horizons	1
Education 5	
With the Asahi 11	
Posting and travel overseas 16	
The Tōhō Jiron 19	
Approach to politics 21	
2 In the front line for party liberalism	24
Adjustment to party politics 31	
The feud with Tanaka 34	
The Minseitō 39	
Breakaway 43	
3 Liberalism sacrificed to national solidarity	48
The Kokumin Dōmei 53	
National action and the Tōhōkai 57	
Relations with the military 65	
4 Staking all on Japan's world mission	70
The global crisis: China, the Axis and the Military 74	
Development of the Tōhōkai 80	
Participation in the Early IRAA 87	
Into the Pacific War—Retreat to Restorationism 92	
5 A final stand for survival with honour	100
The last round 105	
Reflections	115
Notes	122
Bibliography	127

Preface

This book is the outcome of studies and reflections going back to my own experiences in the Pacific War and its aftermath and maintained in the course of subsequent academic activities. More immediately it is based on a thesis submitted to the University of Melbourne. For help leading to its present form, I feel most fundamentally indebted to Mr Charles Bavier, a scholar and gentleman adventurer under whom I studied during the war and who was a long-term resident and devoted student of Japan, latterly in the *Kyōto Shimbun* in the years before his death in 1976. More immediately I would like to express appreciation to Professor Harold Bolitho of Monash University for fruitful discussion; to Professor Hayashi Shigeru, formerly of Tokyo University, for general guidance and help in obtaining source materials; and to Professor Nakano Yasuo of the Ajia University, both for help in studies on his father and for subsequent illuminating contacts on various themes.

The number of brief unacknowledged quotations appearing in the text are all drawn from works listed in the bibliography, chiefly standard works and biographies.

Introduction

Since the Second World War, revulsion against the extreme nationalism which animated the Axis nations has tended, both within and outside them, to overshadow attempts to understand all the underlying factors. This particularly applies in the case of Japan where, although the basic forces propelling the nation towards war resembled those operating in Europe, the developments they triggered were very different.

It is true that broad similarities occur in the stresses to the social order precipitated by the First World War and culminating in the Great Depression. There was also a comparable reaction against the Marxist type of solution and a consequent search for salvation on the basis of traditional ideals, some supra-national when involving religious or broad cultural systems but in the main national when the state's survival or autonomy was felt to be threatened. As the prospect or appeal of an international reconstruction on Marxist lines faded, national goals remained the only viable framework for action, even though plans for national salvation in the name of traditional values needed to be strengthened by drawing on elements of Marxist strategy.

Yet the detailed course of events was strikingly different between Japan and Europe. Whereas the European movements usually grouped as fascist successfully mobilised mass followings to establish single-party dictatorships, the parallel groundswell in Japan for national salvation and 'renovation' failed to achieve anything like this, so that the common use of the term 'fascism' to describe both the renovationist movement and the adjustments made by the ruling Establishment stretch the term beyond any descriptive utility. The indigenous term 'renovationist right' (*kakushin uyoku*) has some justification in that the basic appeal was to national values and interests, though it leads to a confusing overlap with elements described as 'right wing' which essentially supported the existing social order.

The reasons for the overall failure of the Japanese renovationist movement lie both in the nature of the Establishment and in that of the movement itself. The former, despite its complex divisions, succeeded in maintaining a politically viable degree of consensus, even if this was at the cost of finally diverting conflict to the international arena. The latter, despite a fairly wide spectrum of support including elements in the Establishment, utterly failed to produce any effective unification on the basis of either leadership or program comparable with European fascism. The most it achieved, apart from some reshaping of the Establishment, was some spectacular violence and an atmosphere of intrigue and agitation, while its constantly fissioning structure steadily removed it from political effectiveness.

In this setting the figure of Nakano Seigō is quite distinctive. As a long term Diet member and a collaborator with some prominent financiers and military men, he probably wielded more influence in the Establishment than any other figure in the renovationist movement, but clearly belongs to it with his boldly innovative proposals and his unusually successful attempts to mobilise mass support by popular oratory and journalism. His career therefore illuminates the complex situation in Japan leading up to the war as well as various facets of Japanese society.

The Establishment that he and the renovationist movement sought to challenge or manipulate centred on the career civil service to which access was gained by passing the Higher Examinations, for which a training in the Imperial University system (chiefly Tokyo University) was in practice necessary. Its status was guaranteed by the authority of the Privy Council and it enjoyed considerable independence from cabinet control. Though extremely clique-ridden, it had some sort of centre in the Imperial Court system, which was the fount of civil honours and gave final approval for cabinet formation. The office of prime minister could be awarded to any subject whom the court's advisers accepted as most politically viable at the time. Parallel with the civil service were the professional armed services also staffed on the basis of academic performance.

These government organs had in turn fostered the development of highly concentrated industrial and financial combines in which recruitment and organisation were based on family ties and patronage and whose political influence steadily expanded with the modernisation of Japanese society. The formal political process centred on the bicameral Diet, in which access to the House of Peers was determined by birth or bureaucratic favour; while in the elected House of Representatives it depended mainly on affiliation to two or three major political parties. These functioned as agencies for complex bargaining and competition between elements of the bureaucracy, big business and the armed services.

Turning to the renovationist forces confronting the Establishment, we find an equally complex situation. One classification of the Right in the broadest sense distinguishes three streams: the strongly traditionalist right of the 'Imperial Way' or 'Pure Japanists', the centre or primitive agrarianist movement and a 'non-Marxist left', advocating various forms of state socialism. A further classification of the two latter elements, according to social origins, traces the resentment of petty entrepreneurs and farmers against bureaucracy and privileged capital as being channelled through four types of right-wing protesters: professional strong-arm men (*sōshi*), malcontents resenting their failure to obtain advancement through the examination system, dissatisfied (or socially aware) young military officers and recanting left wing intellectuals. Regionally, there is a marked concentration of right wing activism between the southwest, mainly Kyushu, and the northeast, the scenes of the most serious disorders surrounding the inauguration of the modern state from the Meiji Restoration of 1868.

The ideological strands figuring most prominently are the official 'family–state' doctrine, rural community ideals and Pan-Asianism—a theme, going beyond pure nationalism, which was sometimes sentimental and sometimes more calculating. General traits in action were a leaning towards terrorism or putchism, a heroic elitist self-image, a mystical or poetic irrationalism and, at least in theory, a moralistic perfectionism whose relationship to the 'Imperial Way' elements in the Establishment is analogous to that seen on the left between Trotskyist idealists and hard-headed Stalinist power holders.

Nakano shared enough of these features, on the surface, to explain his usual inclusion under 'fascism' or the 'renovationist right'. He originated from Kyushu and from the class of small entrepreneurs whose position has always been insecure. He maintained lifelong hostility to the career civil service recruited only through examination, while his next most consistent theme was the crusade to liberate Asia from western imperialism. He also made frequent use of traditionalist rhetoric in patriotic or samurai terms, as well as collaborating at times with reformist elements in the armed services.

However, he differed from the right wing image in more significant ways. Although his heated oratory and his final confrontation with the Tōjō regime has made him an almost legendary figure of revolt, he rejected terrorism as futile. He was also temperamentally alien to purely sentimental or mystical patriotism, always showing great political resourcefulness and staking his hopes on mobilising mass support, first in the cause of liberalism and latterly in the service of aggressive nationalism. Consistently with this, his nationalism was not centred on the Emperor in accordance with the current orthodoxy but was directed to the nation as a whole, though more particularly to the masses whose plebeian soundness and Japaneseness he contrasted with the 'decadence' of the westernised intelligentsia. His patriotism, however, was not narrow, as he readily welcomed ideas from abroad when they served his purposes.

Nakano did not challenge the existing Constitution as directly as many in the renovationist right did, preferring more realistically to try to manipulate it through popular pressure and any other available means. He was chiefly sustained by a perennial conviction that the system as it stood was doomed to early collapse under the stress of unparallelled crisis and that the key to success was to build up alternative organisations and programs as the situation demanded— 'setting in order a national posture which, when a situation is encountered that we will be the only ones capable of handling, will enable us to perform that duty fully.'

The Establishment's apprehensions of him are indicated by the recurrent censoring of his publications as well as close police surveillance of his later activities. In the end the Establishment's resistance and 'counter-renovation' proved intractable to either the popular support or the covert intrigues he was able to pit against it and, facing checkmate, he died by his own hand. His tragedy reflects that of Japan itself in that the course of events could only have been materially changed by some major alteration to the power structure, which Japanese society proved unable to achieve.

Note on sources

Nakano has received very little attention in works in English on the relevant period, as his approaches to effective power were limited, while his career also lacks the violent drama associated with movements resorting to terrorism. The only study in English of any consequence is that by Tetsuo Najita, 'Nakano Seigō and the Spirit of the Meiji Restoration in Twentieth-Century Japan', in J. W. Morley (ed.), *Dilemmas of Growth in Prewar Japan* (1971), which concentrates on his ideological position.

Even in Japan he has not been made the subject of much academic enquiry. Though remaining a fairly well-known figure and in certain quarters rather admired for his celebrated oratory and intense commitment, he is more generally consigned to the mixed class of 'ultranationalists' who are blamed for the disaster of Japan's defeat and whom it is not desired to commemorate. General histories of modern Japan note the highlights in his career, especially his dramatic end, but there is little reference to him in the biographies of one-time associates who achieved greater conventional success, especially those published after the war.

The main source for details on Nakano's career is a group of biographical studies by less prominent associates who to some degree remained loyal to his memory. Their quality naturally varies. Two studies by his former energetic aide in the Diet, Mitamura Takeo, *Why Did Nakano Seigō End His Life?* (1950) and *Record of Warnings* (1953), chiefly give a graphic account of Nakano's last phases, highlighting the writer's own role and sketching all earlier episodes in Nakano's life which could be adduced to portray him as a lifelong opponent of militarism.

The most widely read and vividly written biography is that by his lifelong friend Ogata Taketora, who had a distinguished career in journalism and postwar conservative politics. Having been himself a fairly consistent liberal throughout, Ogata in his *Nakano Seigō the Man* (1951) concentrates on Nakano's earlier liberalistic phase, when the two were close together, and his last 'redeeming' phase of opposition to the Tōjō regime. These phases are illustrated with a selection of notable writings by Nakano, the intervening 'fascist' period being almost ignored.

Nakano's former publicity aide and youth activist, Inomata Keitarō, first wrote two short sketches entitled *Nakano Seigō and the Japanese Militarists* (1951) and *The Tragedy of Nakano Seigō* (1951), also portraying him as a consistent enemy of militarism. However, he later followed these up with an attempt at a definitive biography on behalf of the Seigō Society, *The Life of Nakano Seigō* (1964), which is very full and indeed quite scholarly. He draws widely on members' recollections and on ample documentation but stops short of any attempt at justification and admits finding much that in retrospect is inexplicable, at least in the context of postwar liberalistic attitudes and hindsight in which he was writing.

The one account which is both unrepentant and unrevisionist is that by Nakano's former youth leader Satō Morio, *Nakano Seigō* (1951). He however limits himself to brief introductory notes to an anthology of Nakano's speeches and writings from his 'right wing' period, so complementing Ogata's study which avoids this.

By far the most impressive study by any standard is the massive two-volume biography by Nakano's youngest son Yasuo, who was just old enough to join in his father's last activities, entitled *Nakano Seigō the Statesman* (1971). This does make an impressive attempt to render Nakano at least intelligible. In what amounts to a political, social and economic history of Japan from the Restoration to his father's death, the author thoroughly castigates the governing 'pseudo-elite' and commends his father to the extent that he challenged them in the interests of the nation as a whole. But he concedes that, through impetuousness and a certain shallow activism, his father so misread the situation that in practice he largely came to serve as a demagogue for the military and their allies.

In this book material from these biographies has been used in conjunction with some short sketches of Nakano by others, biographies of associates and official publications covering his and related political activities. Primary sources include a representative range of Nakano's own publications, including key books and pamphlets and his regular writings in his periodicals, as well as speeches in the Diet. Interviews with Nakano's two surviving sons and other close associates also proved useful. They confirm that Nakano left virtually no personal papers.

1
Launched on a world of expanding horizons

Throughout his formative period, the dominant influences on Nakano's development were characteristic of the major centres of western Kyushu which, owing to the circumstances surrounding the overthrow of the feudal order, had seen Japan's most serious civil disturbances during the first decade after the Meiji Restoration of 1868. Although overt insurrection ended with the defeat and death of its most representative and legendary leader Saigō Takamori in the Satsuma Rebellion, resentment and frustration continued to simmer in this region. These found various modes of expression which, though far from consistent, were to affect, with changing emphases, every phase of Nakano's career.

Though in many ways typical of the region, Nakano's native city of Fukuoka was distinguished politically by developing the most important organised expression of this unrest in the form of the partly traditionalist, partly expansionist and in some ways partly radical society known as the Genyōsha—later regarded as the parent body of all the 'ultranationalist' and radical right wing societies active in Japan in the first half of the twentieth century.

Various reasons can be adduced for the distinctive role of the Genyōsha and of Fukuoka itself. On the one hand, the Kuroda fief centred there in premodern times had enjoyed high standing in the world of samurai culture, both for the practice of the martial arts and for Neo-Confucian learning, as represented by the school of Kaibara Ekken, perpetuated in the Shūyūkan academy. On the other hand, originally owing to the city's location at the nearest point to the Asian mainland, it also housed a particularly well-defined and cohesive merchant community in the townsmen's quarter of Hakata which, right through the Edo period, had retained a long-established autonomy under a committee of six annual councillors. The widespread mingling of lower samurai tradition and merchant enterprise in the late Edo period would seem to have been unusually marked there and Nakano's family, as will be seen, were a typical product of this milieu.

Fukuoka nevertheless made an unfortunate start in the modern era. Loyalist activities among a section of samurai and merchants were violently suppressed in a purge of 1866 by the party supporting the Shogunate and the fief soon afterwards faced the triumphant Meiji regime very much under a cloud. Fukuoka as a whole was therefore at a greater disadvantage compared with such adjoining cities as Saga, Kagoshima and Kumamoto which, although equally or more strife-torn, produced a quite disproportionate share of top national leadership for their more successful factions. Fukuoka ultimately became the dominant regional centre of Kyushu owing to the adjacent mineral resources and the dynamic qualities displayed by its citizens, but only after a persistent struggle against political disadvantage and central Zaibatsu exploitation, which undermined much local enterprise before a certain equilibrium was reached. This whole situation bred political extremism and a local solidarity perhaps unusual even for Japan—a factor appearing constantly in Nakano's career. This, together with other effects of the interaction of equally strong samurai and merchant traditions, also seems to explain the Genyōsha's greater effectiveness as compared with the purely feudalistic and less rationally directed protest movements which were the rule elswhere in Kyushu.

Among the various strands in the Genyōsha tradition itself, the earliest derived from the second major fief school, the Kandōkan, which was a centre of heterodox Confucian studies, in contrast with the orthodoxy of the Shūyūkan. Another was associated with the martyred loyalist Hirano Kuniomi, who had been one of the extreme Restorationists associated with Maki Izumi of nearby Kurume. An early organised expression of such elements after the Restoration was the Kyōshisha (Society for Rectifying Aims), a body affiliated with the nationwide Popular Rights Movement which had arisen as one expression of dissatisfaction with the new oligarchic and modernising regime. The Popular Rights Movement was an ambiguous blend of elements, some favouring modernisation along more liberal lines but others tending towards reaction against modernisation, partly reflecting persisting feudal attitudes found in most classes and partly stemming from anti-Western feelings provoked by the unequal treaties. The Kyōshisha group shared all these elements.

Some of its members, including Tōyama Mitsuru and Shintō Kiheita, were imprisoned on suspicion of implication in the rising of

Maebara Issei in Chōshū, but at least this saved them when other members of the Kyōshisha joined an unsuccessful attack on Fukuoka castle in sympathy with the Satsuma rebels, as a result of which over 100 were killed or executed. Surviving dissidents amalgamated into a new group called the Kōyōsha (Sun-facing Society) which, in 1881, was renamed the Genyōsha (Genkai Sea Society), adopting three articles of association proclaiming veneration for the Imperial House, love of the nation and defence of popular rights. In 1889 one of its members attacked and crippled Foreign Minister Okuma in retaliation for his conciliatory handling of negotiations for treaty revision, also taking his own life.

In the following years, this anti-Western drive developed into support for nascent Chinese nationalism as represented by Sun Yatsen—partly with the aim of fostering a joint resistance to Western dominance and partly in the hope of establishing a new order on the mainland superior in terms of traditional values to the modernising oligarchy in Japan.

Should this program fail, there remained the alternative object of establishing Japanese power in China in competition with the West—a precedent being found in Saigō's earlier advocacy of war with Korea for this type of reason. In either case, Japanese interests would be served and, in particular, those of enterprises based on Fukuoka, which remained Japan's greatest centre of agitation for involvement on the continent—a tangible symbol of this concern often being found in the still surviving wall built there to repel the Mongols in the thirteenth century. So the Genyōsha developed a peculiar ambiguity between support for a 'chivalrous' and traditionalist Pan-Asianism and for a modern Japanese imperialism, comparable with the dichotomy between liberalism and reaction in its popular rights aspect.

In terms of political action, its modernising aspect was represented by its second head, the coal mining operator Hiraoka Kōtarō, who had fought under Saigō but later, as a rising industrialist, became a Diet member and almost went bankrupt giving financial support for the popularly based Ōkuma Cabinet of 1898. In contrast, the outstanding exponent of reactionary extremism (as well as the major champion of Pan-Asianism) was Tōyama, who is quoted as having disparaged the Constitution as merely the work of Itō Hirobumi, the leading oligarch, whom he held in low esteem.[1] Tōyama preferred to speak in terms of the traditionalist ideal of 'popular welfare under the Emperor' (*Ikkun bammin ron*) guaranteed by direct imperial rule—a conception, partly Confucian and partly Shinto in origin, occurring in the ideology of Restorationists like Maki, Hirano and, most notably, Saigō. In time this conception developed into an ideology of protest which is best described as Restorationism, though many of its themes tend to overlap with those of the official nationalist creed. Tōyama was, however, far from being a pure idealist, as he financed his political activities by such means as securing and selling mining rights, largely to central Zaibatsu interests and apparently by high-handed methods.

His ideological ambivalences came to the surface in the election of 1892, notorious for government violence against the rising liberal parties. Despite his earlier enmity for the clan oligarchy, he found the new, non-samurai phase of the liberal movement even more repellent and particularly resented the parties' opposition to military spending—a precondition for strong action on the continent. He therefore threw the weight of Genyōsha terrorism behind the government and the same pattern was repeated throughout Kyushu, which was the only region where the pro-government party, the Chūō Club, gained a decisive success. But Tōyama was dissatisfied with the resulting political situation and later shifted to Tokyo to pursue obscure intrigues on the extremist penumbra of politics, where he became the supreme patriarch—sometimes in league with sections of the Establishment, sometimes fostering violence against 'traitorous' elements within it, but always inexorably opposed to the liberal and proletarian movements.

Soon after Saigō's death, Tōyama had visited his family and obtained from them a copy, annotated in Saigō's own hand, of the *Senshindō Tōki* of Ōshio Heihachirō, a noted hero of the heterodox school of Confucianism founded by Wang Yang-ming. Oshio had died leading an insurrection at Osaka in 1837 on behalf of the destitute townspeople. His school of thought, which in its distinctive Japanese development is best referred to by its naturalised name Yōmeigaku, denies the orthodox doctrine of objective norms in favour of the principle of an infallible intuition, subjectively inherent in anyone with perfect sincerity, of the right course to take in the infinite variety of possible circumstances. This has customarily been regarded as the dominant ideology of most of the noted forerunners of the Restoration such as Sakuma Shōzan, Yoshida Shōin, Takasugi Shinsaku, Yokoi Shōnan and Saigō. Although doubt has been cast on its importance, it is at least well attested in the case of Saigō and through his influence may well have been over-emphasised in the historiography of the Restoration. For the same reason it also figures prominently in the Genyōsha tradition, more particularly through Tōyama. Besides, it was also a congenial doctrine in that, while drawing on the general stock of Confucian moralism, it implied no commitment to any statically defined principles, enjoining only the unreserved translation into action of one's duty as one perceives it. It was therefore well suited to such a body as the Genyōsha, with its ambiguities of theory united only by a commitment to activism. It also had a special appeal to individuals of an impetuous or non-conformist temperament, as is clearly indicated in a defining statement in a late work of Nakano's:

> How can we conserve our energy by grasping the essentials? Rather than chase round after individual phenomena, investigating things here and there, it is better to polish and clear the lucid mirror in one's own heart. Rather than carry round a clouded and distorted mirror, endeavouring to use it to illuminate all objects, the basic principle of learning must be to wipe away the clouds on this mirror, releasing the light of its inherent clarity, and illumine all things without omission whether as right or wrong, good or evil, beautiful or ugly.[2]

It was for such reasons, relating both to his Genyōsha associations and to his own temperament, that Nakano tended, through all the varied phases of his career, to define his position in terms of Yōmeigaku.

Education

Though Nakano was apparently never a formal member of the Genyōsha, influences of this kind were exerted on him in various ways. He was born in 1886 as the eldest son of a certain Taijirō who claimed samurai descent on rather slender grounds, as his ancestors had served in the fief in water transport for a stipend of a mere 7.2 *koku* (the equivalent of 35 bushels of rice per annum). But he was an admirer of Saigō and maintained his claim to a samurai heritage by such gestures as constructing model battlefields, illustrating scenes from the warrior classics, during the Bon (All Souls) Festival.

After the commutation of samurai stipends, the family had set up as pawnbrokers and were fairly prosperous until Nakano had passed his teens. He was originally given the name of Jintarō and his birth was followed over a few years by those of two sisters, Teru and Mura, then of two brothers, Taisuke and Hideto. All of these later maintained close relations with their eldest brother, who continued to exercise the leadership and responsibility for them ordained by tradition.

Jintarō was sent to a local primary school soon after turning five and, after four years there, was transferred to the senior section of the primary school attached to the Fukuoka Normal School. After a further four years, he commenced secondary school studies at the Shūyūkan, now reorganised on more modern lines.

The Saigō cult was also prevalent among his schoolfellows, who always treated Saigō as the hero in their war games and were more enthusiastic about attending the Genyōsha's memorial services for the fallen rebels than those held officially for the government side.[3] The most significant and enduring agent of Genyōsha influence on Nakano was, however, his Chinese Classics master at the senior primary school, Shibata Bunjō, who was Tōyama's nephew. As Tōyama was usually in Tokyo by this time, Nakano met him only later, but from an early stage developed a close relationship with Shibata, who remained one of his closest confidants throughout his career.

Shibata describes Nakano as one of his three star pupils, the others being Shindō Shintarō, who later figured in the Manchuria Volunteer Force guerillas during the Russo–Japanese War, and Ogata Taketora[4], who became Nakano's most consistent personal friend, despite long ideological differences. Ogata came of a family long associated with Dutch learning and had absorbed liberal tendencies which persisted throughout his distinguished career in journalism and later politics.

Shibata imparted to Nakano some degree of taste for classical Chinese lore and the effects on Nakano's rhetoric remain marked. Although he hardly acquired what might be described as serious scholarship in this field, at least until quite late in life, he built up a stock of themes from this source which he regularly and effectively used as pegs on which to hang arguments on current issues. Ogata comments that Confucian idealism made Nakano prone to disillusionment with real life associates[5] but it might be more accurate to say that it provided rationalisations for criticising them, which Nakano was always quick to do. Ogata, like all other sources, stresses his habitual impetuousness.

At the Shūyūkan, where the curriculum laid equal emphasis on the Confucian classics and the martial arts, Nakano at first took more interest in the latter. Students were required to specialise in either judo or fencing and this choice had become linked with an ideological difference. The judo enthusiasts formed a militaristic faction (*budanha*) and the fencers a civilianist faction (*bunjiha*)—these being two categories into which it is customary to classify historical characters. The two most prominent contemporary examples were respectively General Yamagata Aritomo, father of the modern Japanese Army, and Itō Hirobumi, framer of the Meiji Constitution—both members of the dominant Chōshū clique. Nakano chose judo and the attitudes going with it, as well as showing a great interest in riding horses.

Nakano later recalled a scene in which the Principal, a graduate of the progressive Sapporo Agricultural College, attacked the judo faction's attitudes. Once, when this master gave Nakano's class a short

English test, not one could read what he had written on the blackboard. At this, he angrily rebuked them, saying: 'What's this? Aren't you "sons of Kyushu" (*Kyūshū danji*)? I thought the sons of Kyushu had solider qualities, but what about your performance here? Is this your heroism, Genyōsha style? What is this Genyōsha, anyway? Your antics are nothing but outdated fool's heroics. Look at the way you strut—is that how judo players are supposed to walk?' He concluded by pointing out that modern scientific education also produced superior weapons.[6]

In his first year at the Shūyūkan, Nakano received a leg injury while practising this sport which subsequently grew worse and caused him serious trouble in later years, also leading to his rejection for military service. Even at the outset, it necessitated his missing so many lessons that he was forced to repeat his first year at this school.

In 1903, his fifth year there, he took a leading part in establishing a students' centre for practising the martial arts called the Shimbukan. This had no formal owner or regular instructor, and was built and maintained jointly by its users, who would take private lessons elsewhere and pass on or practise their skills among themselves. In raising funds for this project, Nakano obtained help from the Genyōsha leader Hiraoka, and, at a later stage, Tōyama.

Another such venture, showing more direct Genyōsha influence, was Nakano's organising, as an auxiliary organ to the Shimbukan, a club called the Gennankai (South of Genkai Sea Society). Its purpose was to provide practice in debate and composition and to foster the 'oriental heroic spirit'. In pursuit of this latter aim, its members terrorised 'frivolous and dandyish' students and opposed the trend away from traditional to modern sports. The club met weekly at Nakano's home, where his mother, a strong-willed woman who seems likely to have sympathised with its aims, supplied refreshments. The members also circulated their writings among themselves.[7]

Nakano's interests became somewhat more literary in his later years at the Shūyūkan, partly through the stimulus of writing for a magazine for its students and alumni, the *Dōsōkai Zasshi*. This was started in his third year by the Chinese classics master, Masuda Hiroyuki, in order to combat effeminate or 'decadent' literary fashions (meaning the current trend to romanticism or naturalism) by encouraging a more 'virile' style of composition. Nakano was assigned the task of writing a piece on the local hero, Kikuchi Taketoki, who had defended the cause of the Southern Court in the succession dispute in the fourteenth century. His performance was so praised by Masuda that he began to consider a literary career, which appealed to him more than commerce or public office.

Thirteen pieces by Nakano appeared in this magazine over the next five years. From 1903 he wrote under the new name of Masakata, meaning 'true and firm', which he had adopted in samurai style to supersede his childhood name of Jintarō. This name later came to be read in its Sino-Japanese pronunciation Seigō—apparently in the 1920s, as the English tables of contents in his first periodical the *Tōhō Jiron* show his name as 'M. Nakano'. His mother continued to call him Masakata until his death.

His writings in the magazine tended to reflect Genyōsha-type trends towards expansionism and militarism. In his last article written while at the Shūyūkan, he expressed hope that the current war against Russia would restore Japan's best qualities, countering the adulation of Western culture as reflected in the individualistic and emancipist literature of naturalism. However, he dissociated himself from those who regarded Western culture as wholly harmful, arguing that Japan might still derive benefit from it through discrimination. This blend of emotional traditionalism with a degree of tempering modern realism remained characteristic of Nakano throughout his life—in varying proportions but always distinguishing him from the purely emotional or mystical posture of the most extreme right.

His understanding and acceptance of modernisation were naturally stimulated when, after graduating from the Shūyūkan, he enrolled at the prestigious private university of Waseda in April 1905. His choice of this university is attributed by one source to a conscious rejection of the national universities identified with the Establishment, and by another as related to a weakness in mathematics. In the political science course in which he enrolled, his interest was particularly aroused by the lectures of the well-known legal scholar, Ukita Kazutami, on Napoleon and liberalism and by those on economics by Shiozawa Masasada, which included the reading of English texts such as Ely's *Social Economy* and covered the theories of List and late nineteenth century 'cathedral (or academic) socialism'.

Nakano already showed signs of strong ambitions for a career in which such studies might be turned to account. For example, on the occasion of the President's speech of welcome to new students in which he quoted his own habits as an example to follow, Nakano privately commented, 'I'm not one to be satisfied with your level of success!' He later persuaded the younger Ogata to join him at Waseda and contemplated an active political career for the two of them in combination. He did not, however, show any interest in debating or public speaking, for which he later became noted. He did not participate in the mock parliaments which were used to train students in these arts and once challenged an enthusiast by saying, 'Do you think the world can be won by eloquence? Look at Inukai! Look at Ozaki!' These were two of the most prominent Popular Rights leaders of the day.

One means of making social contacts was provided by his participation in the Chikuzen Gakuyūkai, an association of students from Fukuoka, headed by the former daimyo Marquis Kuroda. He also formed relationships with a number of Chinese, chiefly students, whom he helped in such ways as supplying notes, in exchange for financial assistance when he or his fellow boarders needed it. One of these was Lin Ch'ang-min, who later held ministerial office in the post-revolutionary Chinese government and with whom Nakano maintained contact in relation to his many interests in China. Another was Ting Chien-hsiu from Manchuria, who later became a minister in the Manchukuo government. Nakano also mixed with exiled revolutionaries, whose activities centred on the newspaper *Min Pao*. Its office was used by the T'ung-meng-hui Society, led by Sun Yat-sen and Huang Hsing, whom Nakano came to know.

In the summer holidays of 1908 Ting took him on a visit to his native place. The main incident in this trip was a visit at Dairen to the Pan-Asianist scholar Kaneko Sessai, who seems to have been widely respected among traditionally oriented right wing circles. A postwar work by a representative right wing radical, Homma Kenichirō of Mito, who was a late associate of Nakano's, entitled *Banish the Bureaucrats* (1952), is dedicated both to Tōyama and to Kaneko. However, Kaneko seems to have been more of a scholar than Tōyama and more genuinely interested in achieving a true understanding between Chinese and Japanese although, as he died in 1925, he did not have to face the stern test of the later conflicts between them. In any case, Nakano came to show the highest esteem for him as a mentor, both during his lifetime and in retrospect—more consistently than he did for Tōyama or, indeed, anyone else, as he frequently changed loyalties and revised estimates of character. Their first encounter, though on the surface unpromising, set the keynote of their relationship, which was cast in the traditional pattern of stern but kindly master and difficult but responsive disciple.

Kaneko, who had qualifications both in classical Chinese and in Western learning, had worked among the natives of Taiwan and later as a senior linguist in the Russo–Japanese War, at the end of which he settled at Dairen, resolved to 'build a Spiritual Japan in Manchuria'. To this end he had established a private school for both Chinese and Japanese youths called the Shintōsha (Orient Advancement Society) Academy and won so much support among the local Chinese that they provided funds for the establishment of a Chinese language newspaper, the *T'ai-tung Jih-pao*, for which he himself wrote.

When Nakano and Ting called on him, Kaneko was pleased to see the pair of youths, Japanese and 'Manchurian', travelling together and spoke to them encouragingly about future accord between their countries. In the course of conversation, however, he happened to ask where they were staying and, on being told that they were at the Liaotung Hotel, his manner abruptly changed. He upbraided them for luxurious living, saying that there was grave concern for the future of the Orient if this was how its youth behaved.

Actually, they had been staying at a low class Chinese inn under trying conditions until a local journalist and Waseda graduate took pity on them and treated them to better class accommodation. But Kaneko gave them no chance to explain and they left with a protest that this was no way to treat new acquaintances.[8] Yet Ting later confessed to being impressed by him, and Nakano's imagination was also apparently caught by his old world Spartan asceticism, to judge by their later relationship.

On Nakano's return to Tokyo, he shifted to a boarding house mainly catering for Chinese, his aim being to gain practice in Chinese conversation, as many of them knew little Japanese. Clearly his visit to the mainland had captured his interest in that direction. When his family moved to Tokyo after the failure of their business through excessive support for a relative who went bankrupt, they took a house into which he also moved, at the same time accommodating a Chinese boarder of good family whose rental provided an important source of income. This boarder had been staying with Prince Konoe Atsumaro, a prominent advocate of Sino–Japanese solidarity, and had been introduced to the Nakano family through Inukai Tsuyoshi, another champion of Pan-Asianism—though in his case approached from the standpoint of party liberalism.

The family's only other regular source of income was the monthly fee of ¥30 which Seigō earned from about this time as a regular writer for the traditionalist journal *Nihon oyobi Nihonjin* (Japan and the Japanese) brought out by Miyake Setsurei. From this time and throughout his journalistic career he used the regular pen-name Kōdō (sometimes extended to Kōdō Ujin and at times replaced by jocular pseudonyms). This was derived from the fencing name of an older schoolfellow, pronounced similarly but written differently, using the same 'dō' as in Inukai's pen-name 'Bokudō'.

Some occasional financial help was also obtained from Tōyama. He had meanwhile been associated with Prince Konoe in the Firm Foreign Policy Alliance (*Taigaikō Dōshikai*)—later renamed the Alliance for Action on Russia (*Tai Ro Dōshikai*)—then with the veteran liberal Kōno Hironaka in the violent riots protesting against the terms of peace with Russia in 1905.

In his last year or so at Waseda, Nakano did little formal course work, being chiefly occupied with writing or with extra-curricular reading. He also, in company with his fellow student and lifelong associate, Kazami Akira of Mito, who had been born on the same day as himself, frequented the Rōninkai (Outlaws Society), a branch of the Genyōsha and its earlier offshoot the Kokuryūkai (Amur River Society). The Rōninkai in the 1920s became the spearhead of antiliberal violence but at this stage was mainly concerned with action on the continent. Nakano's final examination results were therefore not particularly distinguished, though his graduation thesis on China was praised by Professor Ukita as showing 'uncommon talent'. Its contents do not appear to be available. His graduation took place in July 1909.

With the *Asahi*

Professor Ukita retained an interest in Nakano after his graduation and helped him to obtain employment, first, briefly, with the *Nichinichi* newspaper and then with the more influential *Asahi*. Nakano did not, of course, regard journalism as his final ambition but as a stepping stone to politics. He is quoted as writing to a friend about his appointment, 'With this as a base, I should in time be able to turn it to some account in the political field.' This was a course that Inukai had followed and which Nakano quotes him as recommending. It also had the effect of inclining him throughout his career to emphasise the role of publicity in the political process.

From early in 1911 he was placed under Yugeta Seiichi in the Reportorial Department, controlling all political and economic news. Yugeta, who shared Ukita's Dōshisha University background, formed a close relationship with his protege and encouraged him to indulge in uninhibited political comment, sometimes under pseudonyms. The body of writings produced under Yugeta's patronage indicates that many of Nakano's lifelong attitudes had already been formed in the interaction between his Genyōsha background and Waseda liberalism. The literary quality of his earlier output is also described as never having been quite equalled in Nakano's later writing—the reason being that he came to concentrate on largely improvised oratory, which also moulded his written form of expression.

He began with a series of biting critiques on the current political scene under the title 'Politicians in and out of Office' (*Chōya no Seijika*). These opened with an attack on the agreement reached by General Katsura and Prince Saionji (the respective proteges of Yamagata and Itō) to serve in rotation as prime minister when cabinet changes were necessary—an arrangement compared by Nakano to notorious contemporary rigged wrestling matches.

He went on to consider eight obvious candidates for future championship in the political ring, but discarded them all. The three most important were the two major party leaders, Hara of the Seiyūkai and Inukai of the Kokumintō, together with General Terauchi, next in line for leadership of the dominant Chōshū clique. Hara was credited with force of character and resilience but judged incapable of carrying through any grand design. Inukai received some ambiguous praise, being hailed as the 'complete oppositionist politician—the hero of a subterranean tragedy who will never rise above it'.[9] In confronting the clan oligarchy, 35 years of opposition by mere debate had not undermined its power.

Terauchi received the most caustic treatment—Nakano protesting that he had to include this 'mediocre soldier' in his series only because of the failure of the politicians to end clan dominance. Terauchi was condemned for filling the higher Army ranks from aristocratic and wealthy circles rather than sturdier elements of society—a populist line that Nakano ever afterwards pursued.[10]

This series proved popular enough to be published in book form with introductions by Yugeta and Ukita. The friendly Chief Editor Ikebe is said to have warned Nakano that, if he entertained political ambitions, he should take care not to make too many enemies. But such advice was ignored—an early sign of Nakano's lifelong expectation that the established political structure had no future, so that deference to it would not pay any dividends in the long run.

Nakano was later joined on Yugeta's staff by two friends, Ogata and Ōnishi Itsuki, both of Fukuoka. Ogata remained with the *Asahi* until late in the Second World War, becoming chief editor. On joining the staff, he gained the impression that Nakano, while towering above his colleagues in ability, was at the same time isolated from them. This situation arose from (and was aggravated by) his marked attitude of self-assurance, arising from Yugeta's favour and the public interest shown in his writings. Ogata comments that a fleet must advance at the pace of the slowest ship and, if the flagship uses its speed to outstrip the others, disorder results—or else the slower ships keep their own counsel and form a common front.[11]

For the time being, Nakano now became chiefly involved in Chinese questions. In December 1911, when Yamagata's stand against the revolution there was supported by the ultranationalist writer Tokutomi Sohō in his *Kokumin Shimbun*, Nakano replied vigorously in a series called 'The Conflagration on the Further Shore' (*Taigan no Kasai*). In it he argued that the only possible effect that China's example could have on Japan would be a desirable reawakening to its 'essential national character' (*kokutai*) by the overthrow of the clan oligarchy and the reform of the corrupt parties. Following this clash, it was only very late in Nakano's career that he and Tokutomi drew close together—one measure of the realignments that had intervened.

Soon afterwards Nakano accompanied to Shanghai, as reporter, a mission led by Tōyama and Inukai which was intended to back the revolution as well as turn it to some advantage. They were supported by General Miura Gorō, a Chōshū Privy Councillor of the anti-Yamagata faction, who had also just cooperated with them in securing the election to the Diet of Kojima Kazuo, a journalist sympathetic to this cause. Kojima soon came to serve as Inukai's right-hand man in the Diet and was for a time very close to Nakano, ultimately surviving the Second World War with considerable political influence.

The mission to China had the two main aims of curbing the lawless activities of Japanese adventurers there and of presenting a proposal by Mitsui and Kyushu mining interests for joint Sino–Japanese management of the Hanyehp'ing coal and steel works. In Shanghai the party was met by the revolutionary commander-in-chief, Huang Hsing, and President-elect Sun Yat-sen, both of whom Nakano had known while at Waseda. The latter now impressed him (not too favourably) as a 'Western gentleman', in contrast with Huang's 'Oriental hero type'.[12] Nakano was also reunited with his former fellow student Lin Ch'ang-min on a visit to Nanking for the inauguration of the republic.

On returning to Japan in January 1912, he wrote a number of articles on his experiences, favouring the revolutionary side and justifying his stand rather simplistically in the terms:

> Since I favour freedom in government, I do not support despotism by a section of oligarchs and party men. So, looking abroad and observing the situation in our neighbour country, I detest the despotic rule of the Manchu court and welcome the liberal thought of the revolutionary party.[13]

The experience had, however, been a significant one and is often mentioned in Nakano's later frequent pronouncements on China to establish his authority in this field.

From October 1912, he began another major series of articles written under his usual pen-name Kōdō and entitled 'A Study of the Popular Rights Movement in the Meiji Period' (*Meiji Minken Shiron*), which was also later published in book form. The idea had been suggested by Yugeta because the recent death of Emperor Meiji provided a suitable occasion to review the achievements of his reign. Apart from consulting Japanese sources and interviewing figures with firsthand knowledge in preparing to write it, Nakano read

Machiavelli's *History of Rome* and Macaulay's *History of England*.

The introduction condemns the corruption of contemporary politics and, using the new Emperor's reign title, calls for a 'Taishō Restoration' to correct it. The Meiji Restoration is described as an 'unprecedented glorious event' which had changed the 'form of government' (*seitai*) from a 'caste-based state' to a 'citizen state'. This formula contrasts with that of Kita Ikki, the most celebrated ideologue in the later renovationist right, who in his *Kokutairon and Pure Socialism* (1906) had described the 'citizen state' as a new 'form of state' (*kokutai*), a more dangerous assertion. Nakano's choice of terms shows that, despite his hostility to the power-holders and their methods, he was not prepared to attack the basic ideology associated with the Meiji constitution, as Kita had done. His proposals for 'renovation' always related to modes of restructuring possible within that framework.

The Restoration, he claims, had been achieved by a 'national movement which washed away the evils of the former oligarchy with the blood of countless martyrs'. In the first phase, the bureaucratism of later times had not yet arisen and the path to political advancement and expression was open to all in a national unity dedicated to matching the West in culture and power—a description which at least indicates the situation which Nakano would have liked to prevail.

The leadership met its first major crisis in the Korea question of 1873, which defined the division between the truly 'populist party of justice', led by Saigō, and that of 'bureaucratic expediency' led by Iwakura. In Nakano's view, the real drive towards progress arises not from leadership but from the stimulus of popular pressure, which Saigō represented more faithfully because at that stage opposition to the unequal treaties demanded a demonstration of strength on the international scene. His defeat opened the way to domination by the Chōshū-centred oligarchy which has since prevailed.

The next phase of protest, seen in the disturbances at Fukushima and others associated with the radical wing of the Popular Rights Movement, is judged as being of a 'lower grade' than the samurai risings in Kyushu, though it made its contribution. But the form the party movement had assumed by the introduction of the Constitution made the Diet a mere organ for bargaining with the oligarchy, which resulted in compromise, sycophancy and corruption.

When the futility of this pattern was grasped, it led to a brief 'second rejection of compromise' (after Saigō's) in which the parties 'stormed the citadel of the oligarchy' to form the Ōkuma-Itagaki Cabinet of 1898. Its disintegration was followed in turn by General Yamagata's return to power, while Itō's reply in forming the Seiyūkai led merely to the alternation between Katsura and Saionji.

While Nakano was finishing this series, Japan was undergoing the Taishō Political Crisis, in which the symbiosis between oligarchy and party leaders for a time broke down, leading to an upsurge of popular protest. So Nakano closed on a topical note, hoping the crisis would produce a third phase of no compromise:

> If the oligarchy is swept away, we must not neglect to reform the parties simulaneously. Anything like the cleansing of the tainted blood of the oligarchy with the equally impure blood of party cliques is what we must most beware of.[14]

He had been taking part in the 'Movement to Defend the Constitution', which no doubt seemed an example of the popular pressure which he professed to see as the mainspring of progress. He joined in action by journalists as well as in mass agitation, enthusiastically supporting it in his press reports and idolising its two stars, Inukai and Ozaki Yukio. Regarding his output of writing in this period, he is said to have remarked that he wrote 'as if he had taken a purgative'. It included a series of emotional open letters to the leading figures in the complex struggle.

The first, addressed to the villain Katsura, described him as the mainstay of the Elder Statesmen's domination, since 'only by making use of Your Excellency's presence can they continue to form a barrier between Sovereign and People, making our Constitution a dead letter'. Nakano was, however, apparently confident that the oligarchy's days were now numbered.

Among other letters, those addressed to Inukai and Ozaki expressed the most ardent support. Inukai in particular was placed on the highest pedestal and urged to continue the struggle until the 'constitutional paradise' was achieved. A recurrent refrain enjoined him to take care of his health, implying the great value of his life to his country.

Another, written to Hara after his agreement to back a government led by Admiral Yamamoto of the rival Satsuma clique, portrayed him as the supreme traitor, 'the worm in the lion's body'. 'Until we see your death agony, we will not put up the spears of our attack'.

In May 1913, these letters were published under the title *Shichikin Hasshō* (a classical Chinese reference to 'giving a fair fight'), carrying a preface to the effect that the titles employed were used as a matter of form and did not necessarily indicate respect. Inukai and Ozaki were addressed as *sensei* (respected elder) out of true respect, while Hara was addressed as *kun* (a plain male form of address) because he neither had a formal title nor deserved anything better.

Another feature of this work worth nothing is a defence of Ozaki from a charge of *lèse majesté*, which arose from his attack on Katsura's use of imperial rescripts, so implying that a rescript could be in error. In a famous scene in the Diet, he had described the government's tactics as 'hiding themselves behind the Throne and shooting at their political enemies from this secure ambush. The Throne is their rampart. Rescripts are their missiles'.

Nakano described as 'barbarian' the idea that the Emperor is infallible or superhuman. The subject should regard him as the head of a 'nation family'—an essentially human figure, though still compatible with his role as conceived under the Constitution. Nakano preserved this stand throughout all his future evolution, in contrast with the more mystically inclined elements in the right.

Posting and travel overseas

The anti-climax which followed the heady and hopeful drama of the Taishō Crisis led to a reaction in many quarters against the more radical advocates of reform and in his relations with the *Asahi* staff Nakano suffered from this because of the extreme commitment and self-assurance with which he, with Yugeta's backing, had pressed the campaign. This also compounded a series of bitter factional disputes which had long riven the *Asahi* staff and in which Nakano had joined with his usual vigour.[15] The acuteness of the resulting tension is indicated by the solution adopted—Nakano being posted to Seoul for a year on the understanding that he could then visit Europe for study.

Before leaving he married Tamiko, the daughter of Miyake Setsurei for whom he had written while at Waseda. Her mother, the writer Kaho, is said to have doubted that a Waseda man could make a fit match for her daughter, but matters were arranged through the good offices of Tōyama and Kojima. The couple soon left for Seoul and their first son, Katsuaki, was born there.

On arrival Nakano, as indicated in regular letters to Kojima, felt largely isolated. His first major story was a topical article entitled 'A Glimpse of the Korean Countryside'—his first piece in vernacular style, which was now coming into general acceptance. Later in the year, he accompanied a group of Korean businessmen on a survey of Manchuria preparatory to a commercial conference at Dairen, which he described in the series 'Sketches of Travel in Manchuria'. In this he expressed a mixture of resentment at Western domination (observed in the Customs and the Russian-owned railway) and impatience with Chinese ineffectiveness—a combination that was to lead through varying phases to his final conviction that Japan had to take the solution of China's problems into her own hands.

Our country alone preaches humanity and presses for justice on their behalf. Yet, on the one hand perplexed by the witless 'heroes' of the South and on the other earning ill-will for the sake of the arrogant Yüan Shih-k'ai [dictator in Peking], we are steadily accumulating diplomatic fiascos.[16]

He also commented that, while the Chinese lacked the power to control Manchuria, the Japanese lacked the resolution to fill the gap.

At the end of the year he revisited Kaneko Sessai in Dairen and continued to visit him whenever he could during his tour of duty in Korea, as well as later. He subsequently often referred to Kaneko as his most valued mentor, even adopting the name of Kaneko's school for the one which he himself opened in his last years. It is difficult to see, however, where Kaneko influenced him in specific respects. Nakano quotes him, for example, as advocating independence for Korea, as paternalism would not work—a view which Nakano never accepted. Kaneko also counselled patience with mediocrities—something equally absent from Nakano's attitudes.[17] Kaneko may have had some effect in urging fairness to the Chinese, a policy which long competed for Nakano's support against his growing inclination to prefer the outright domination of China. In essence, however, Nakano's lifelong professions of veneration for Kaneko amount to an example of the long established East Asian pattern by which every thinker is expected to owe final allegiance to one particular master (or guru figure) to whose lineage he counts himself as belonging—as well as having an underlying philosophical commitment, in Nakano's case Yōmeigaku (to which Kaneko also subscribed).

The last and most searching of the series of articles Nakano wrote in Korea, collected in 'Manchuria and Korea as I saw them' (*Waga mitaru Mansen*) (1915), was 'The Governor-General's Administration'. His basic criticism of Governor-General Terauchi was that he had no conception of the principle of 'letting society regulate itself'— rather preferring a despotic regulation from above. Nakano described this as outdated in the complexities of modern society, which can only function satisfactorily by mutual supervision in each field— political, economic, moral and so forth. Instead, under Terauchi, there was no free press; paternalistic economic controls fostered monopolistic privilege; while the military police (*kempeitai*) administration denied Japanese subjects their right to a proper trial.

The colonial administration, so described, seems to foreshadow the bureaucratic totalitarianism which was to prevail in Japan itself a couple of decades later and it is worth noting that Nakano had already formulated something of the line with which he was then to oppose it, as well as both socialism and liberalism, namely the organizing of society by self-regulating groups, bound together by a common ideology of national destiny. This seems to have been suggested by the thought of Inukai, who is described by Kojima as seeking to enlist the support of segments of the population outside the political process. For this purpose he hoped to mobilise occupational groups such as scholars, businessmen, students and workers. Bureaucrats and soldiers, if bold enough, would be invited to participate on their merits.

As Nakano's term in Korea drew to a close, he negotiated with the *Asahi* head office about his future. Though still willing to grant him leave for study, the company was not prepared to meet all expenses. This problem was solved with the help of Kojima, General Miura and Tōyama, who obtained the necessary funds, including maintenance for Nakano's many dependants, from the Fukuoka mine owner Yasukawa Keiichirō. The latter was the father of Nakano's friend Daigorō (formerly of the Gennankai club) and was the regular financier of Tōyama's activities. Nakano set off in March 1915 and Miura's farewell suggests the sort of image that tends to be associated with Nakano—as 'uncouth' but honest, a scorner of social graces and over-intellectualism. 'Now', said Miura, 'when you go over there, mind that you cut a smart figure, just the way they do, even if it's a bit troublesome—right? But when you come back home, be sure you go back to being just your old self!'[18]

During the voyage Nakano was, by his own account, largely preoccupied with the question of colonialism, which affected all regions where his ship called between Japan and Marseilles.[19] Japan's mission, he was convinced, was both to expand its economic activities in this new world and to work towards its emancipation—views which of course reflected those long urged by Tōyama, Inukai and their varied associates.

His stay in Britain—occupying most of his time—far from softening him towards that country, seems to have added an element of personal distaste for things British to an earlier ideological hostility stemming from anti-colonialism and opposition to the oligarchy, whose diplomacy largely rested on the British alliance. A later close colleague, Professor Sugimori Kōjirō of Waseda, recalls that on their first encounter at the Japanese Club in London Nakano was bitterly attacking Japan's hasty participation in the war on the British side.[20]

More personal expressions of distaste were conveyed in his letters home. 'The more I see of the British, the more worthless they seem.' 'Whatever the outcome of the war, this country can only end in collapse ... Politicians, scholars, students—all are worthless.' He even wrote articles to Miyake's journal refuting the pro-British views of Professor Ukita. Although he does not give many concrete reasons for his impressions, he mentions signs of conceit, hypocrisy and meanness in social contacts. On a visit to a military hospital, he was convinced that most of the patients were malingering and observed that they were attended by a crowd of mistresses. British arts and letters also seemed to show signs of decadence. So it would seem that, parallel with Nakano's confidence in the Japanese oligarchy's collapse, he was encouraged to expect a British decline on the international scene—both opening up dramatic opportunities.

Finally, feeling that he had 'graduated' from Europe and eager for action at home, he cut his stay short and in 1916, after a visit to the more accessible continental countries, returned to Japan via the United States.

The *Tōhō Jiron*

There was now little room for him in the *Asahi*, which Yugeta had already left, and at the end of the year he became chief editor of the monthly *Tōhō Jiron*. This had just been established by Higashi Norimasa, former secretary-general of the Japanese Chamber of Commerce in Shanghai, who had employed funds contributed by that body to found the journal 'in the interests of Asia'. By this was meant, judging by its contents, a coverage of international issues independent of official Europe-centred diplomacy and reflecting the interests of circles directly involved in the tangled China situation. Yoshino Sakuzō, and authority on China as well as a prominent liberal, early wrote for it.

In Nakano's account of his appointment, he writes that Higashi had shown interest in his European experiences and valued his political contacts in Japan.[21] His editorial reviews, always strongly critical of the government, constantly strove to promote an awareness of crisis which now, as later, he tried to exploit in the interests of national 'renovation'—though defining this only in the broadest terms. In phrases well-worn again in the 1930s, he claims that under Prime Minister Terauchi 'all traces of politics have been extinguished by bureaucracy in misapplying the principle of national unity', going on to argue that 'real loyalists always have a revolutionary spirit'. What was really needed was a 'mass-based national unity'. In a characteristically elaborate metaphor, he says: 'Stagnation brings decay and decay brings fermentation which finally, without a great and basic renovation, it will be quite impossible to control.'[22]

He suffered some disillusionment with Inukai at this stage, owing to his participation in Terauchi's organ for 'national unity', the Foreign Policy Deliberation Committee (*Gaikō Chōsakai*). Though at first reserving judgement, he later expressed disappointment that Inukai had failed to use it to press any of his long held aims, and explained his failure in terms of his blind hatred of the Kenseikai party ('a religion with him').[23] This party had formed around breakaways from his Kokumintō and had refused to join the Committee.

Nakano naturally gave a good deal of space to China, in regard to which he attacked the Twenty-one Demands—inspired by the 'military clique'—and its legacies. He steadily advocated Japanese mediation between the Peking warlords and the southern republicans, as against Terauchi's financing of the former. He urged that loans and aid to China be considered only on the precondition of China's unification, which he suggested could be achieved under a revival of the original republican constitution based on a system of representative government. On a visit to China he even put this to the Peking dictator Tuan Ch'i-jui. At the same time he still deplored the lack of resolution among the Chinese generally.

He unfavourably compared the confusion and vacillation in China with the dynamism of the Russian revolution with which, from the first, he tended to sympathise, in contrast with the horror shown in most quarters. He denied that Lenin was a German puppet, and portrayed the revolution as having raised Russia from defeat to a role of ideological initiative, inspiring President Wilson's three peace principles of no annexation, no reparations and self-determination.[24] Nakano's initial reactions represented a natural enough analogy to his stands on the Chinese revolution and the Taishō Crisis and, even when the distinctive character of the Soviet regime became clearer, he could still press for understanding with it as a counter to Anglo–American domination. He attacked in the bitterest terms the government's decision, accepted by the Gaikō Chōsakai, to intervene in Siberia, and always afterwards maintained this general approach to Russian questions—one of his most consistent and distinctive political postures.

A concurrent domestic issue with some bearing on the general question of social revolution was the outbreak of the Rice Riots in late 1918. An article Nakano wrote on these, 'In Memory of Ōshio Heihachirō', is also a good example of his habit of framing current issues in terms of Yōmeigaku. In it he argues that any rebel must be judged in terms of his own qualities. An example of the lower kind is provided by those who once rioted in the name of popular rights but, for lack of a clear and sound objective, have now degenerated into the 'running dogs' of power i.e. the *sōshi* or political thugs who long remained a blot on party politics. This judgement of the less rational forms of political violence suggests his later reservations about the right-wing terrorists of the thirties.

Ōshio, had, in contrast, in accordance with the principles of

Yōmeigaku, so identified himself with the whole world that he felt the misdeeds and sorrows of others as infecting him personally and, 'like Saigō', could not rest short of every effort to correct them. He also had high personal standards of the kind now so lacking among many of those radicals classed as 'subversive', whose lives are so debauched that they are totally disqualified to remedy society's ills.[25] The combination here of elements of radicalism with a puritanical adherence to conventional morality remained characteristic of Nakano and later provided a point of contact with European fascism.

Early in 1919 he went to Versailles to cover the Peace Conference for the *Tōhō Jiron*. He had early expressed the hope that there should be no need to fear the effects of the Peace Treaty on Japan's war gains in Shantung and elsewhere because these could be held as 'securities' for bargaining against the colonial powers' relinquishment of their own holdings. He also expressed some hope that Wilson's principle of self-determination might apply in Asia, though in an article written on his way through the United States he showed concern that American idealism might only prove to be a cover for world domination.

Once in Versailles, he was appalled by the Japanese delegation's feeble showing in the face of Chinese attack, under United States guidance, on the Shantung question, as well as by Chinese willingness to combine with the United States against Japan. Claiming to be unable to endure more than a few weeks of the conference, he hurried back to Japan to expose the situation and agitate for the delegation's replacement. He addressed large public meetings—the beginning of his career as a popular orator—and serialised his views in the *Asahi* under the title 'Witnessing the Peace Conference'. The publication of this series in pamphlet form by the *Tōhō Jiron* sold well and increased the journal's circulation from about 2000 to 7000, also making Nakano much better known. Among the wide range of issues discussed, he called on the government to defy the United States regarding the fortification of mandated territories and to win China's acceptance of a 'Far Eastern Monroe Doctrine' (a current slogan) by pointing out the greater evils China had suffered at Western hands.

Approach to politics

This episode marked a clear advance in Nakano's plans to enter politics. He had been working for some time to build up organisational footholds. The *Tōhō Jiron*, of which he had become the company president late in 1918, had early come to serve as the focus for an informal study group called the Tōhōkai (Orient Society)—in later years the name of his own political party—which held monthly meetings on the premises to discuss current affairs over Chinese meals. Members included Mori Kaku and Takagi Rikurō of Mitsui interests in China, military men like Hayashi Senjurō and Araki Sadao, foreign ministry members like the China expert Honda Kumatarō and more personal associates like Miyake, Professor Sugimori and former fellow-student Kazami. Kazami had also become a journalist and had worked for both the *Nichinichi* and the *Asahi*, then moving into independent local journals.

Later in 1918 Nakano joined in forming a mixed discussion group of more radical leanings called the Rōsōkai (Old and Young Society), described as the 'parent body of figures who later played central roles in the renovationist movement'. It included old hands like Oi Kentaro and newer agitators like the Pan-Asianist Ōkawa Shūmei, the agrarianist Gondō Seikyō and the socialist Takabatake Motoyuki, translator of Marx's *Kapital*. After the Versailles conference it was contacted from China by Kita Ikki who, after his early advocacy of socialistic principles, had spent some years in that country under the auspices of the Fukuoka Kokuryūkai and about this time produced his celebrated blueprint for radical social reform after military coup entitled 'Outline Plan for the Reconstruction of Japan' (*Nihon Kaizō Hōan Taikō*). He now wrote to the Rōsōkai's organiser Professor Mitsukawa Kametarō, commending Nakano's views—so beginning a lasting association with Nakano.

Before long, Kita's immediate sympathisers formed their own more extremist society, the Yūzonsha, while Nakano joined a contrasting body, the Kaizō Dōmei (Reconstruction League), dedicated to liberal-type reform within the constitutional structure. It began with journalists who had been at Versailles and included Diet members, as well as Nagai Ryūtarō, than an academic at Waseda. His relationship with Nakano also proved long and significant, the two being generally classed together later as the outstanding orators of interwar politics. The League's platform advocated universal suffrage, a 'democratic' (*mimponteki*) political structure, an end to bureaucratic diplomacy and the recognition of trade unions. Nakano was now well enough established on the fringes of political and financial power to see better prospects in widening the power structure than in challenging it as bluntly as he had done earlier.

The base he had developed now sufficed to gain him election to the Diet. He had first stood as an independent candidate for Fukuoka in 1917, with the backing of Tōyama, Yasukawa and Takagi, the two latter having been associated with mining interests in China. His potential support was, however, split by the rival candidature of Miyagawa Ikkan, backed by the Kokuryūkai—the more pro-government offshoot of the Genyōsha. This body's attitudes are clear from its support of the Siberian Expedition and its use of terror against the rice rioters and their sympathisers.[26] Both Nakano and Miyagawa lost to Matsunaga Yasuzaemon, an outside businessman with wider financial resources who was head of the Kyushu Electricity Association.

In 1920, however, Tōyama arranged for Miyagawa to refrain from standing for election (though he entered the Diet later) and the latter's dramatic announcement of this decision at Nakano's first campaign meeting carried great impact, enabling Nakano to become the sole champion of the traditional Hakata solidarity against outside interests. Nakano's position had also improved through the publicity associated with the Peace Conference, which had at the same time given him valuable experience in vigorous public campaigning. A step had been taken in the direction of mass politics by the Hara Cabinet's reduction of the electoral tax qualification to Y3, which introduced new voters more sympathetic to 'reconstruction' as well as more amenable to Nakano's emotional style. Matsunaga was less adept at this type of campaigning and presented himself as a representative of 'commonsense' against Nakano's sensationalism.

Yasukawa supported Nakano's campaign generously to the extent of ¥150 000, enabling the use of a staff of 300, full page newspaper advertisements and the hiring of a first class hotel as headquarters (though Matsunaga's spending was double this). Nakano also received direct support from Inukai and, though still not joining his party, was classed as a 'pro-Kokumintō independent'. With these factors in his favour, he was elected and entered the Diet confident that his formula of mass appeal and social advancement would work equally well on the national stage.

During his journalistic preparation for a political career, Nakano had developed most of the basic attitudes and arguments on social reconstruction and diplomatic realignment that would reappear with greater force in the 1930s. Their earlier tentative formulation might even be described as a rehearsal for that later phase of his life, though with the paradox that, in a greatly changed context, arguments earlier linked with liberalism would then come to be classed as 'fascism'.

However, he had now become a member of the Diet and, with his gradual adjustment to that role, his primary ideological biases would tend to become restrained or adapted to the practical needs of party politics—a course to be expected in a young radical making good. This is how he might perhaps have remained, if party politics as a whole had not then reached an impasse.

2
In the front line for party liberalism

Having been elected, Nakano became one of the representatives in the Diet of a postwar younger generation of politicians (*shinjin*, *shō-sōha*) who were identified with the new pressures for reform arising in the current environment of ideological ferment and economic instability. Their slogan was 'national reconstruction', in contrast with the mere distribution of patronage which had been the main concern of the established parties in their contest for power with the clan oligarchy.

At the outset Nakano and many of this group remained independent of all three major parties because none of these was free from association with the faults of the existing order, while for a time there seemed to be a real prospect that a new type of political grouping might emerge. Of the major parties, the Seiyūkai, then in power under Hara, was least affected by reformism. The Kenseikai, in order to contest the Seiyūkai's dominance, had been obliged to associate itself with the demand for 'reconstruction' and contained a number of young reformists, for example Miki Bukichi, a later associate of Nakano's. Nagai Ryūtarō, who had also just been elected, soon joined this party, though he also maintained a separate base in the Sea of Japan League of Youth Parties (*Nihonkai Seinentō Remmei*). Nagai was already known as an orator and Nakano was seen as rivalling him in this respect, as indicated by an interjection in Nakano's maiden speech on 10 July 1920, 'He's not as good as Nagai!' But the Kenseikai's tortuous manoeuvres in pressing the central demand for manhood suffrage had so disillusioned the new radicals that the slogans raised on the first May Day Rally in 1920 made no mention of the issue. Inukai's Kokumintō, the other party, though supporting the Kenseikai's efforts, suffered from the twin drawbacks of past compromises and electoral decline.

Nakano's adaptation to practical Diet politics and his development of a more modern political style only progressed gradually. Along with his initial organisational independence, he long retained a tendency to express himself in terms of traditional concepts, as contrasted with the most westernised liberals—Nagai, for example, being also a Christian. To some extent Nakano's utterances were moulded by the tastes of his constituency, dominated by Genyōsha connections. For example, his constituency organisation, the Yūkōkai ('Still Arising Society'—from the saying of the Chinese philosopher Mencius that 'heroes still arise even after the passing of King Wen') was headed by the Genyōsha leader Shintō Kiheita. So we find him even some years later on the anniversary of Saigō's death explaining his support for manhood suffrage in these terms:

> [Nakae] Tōju's spirit in serving the peasants and that of [Saigō] Nanshū in appealing to the sturdy sons of Southern Satsuma represent the same attitude as the Buddha's in joining the company of mendicant ascetics, that of Confucius in starving with his disciples between Ch'en and Tsai and that of Jesus in preaching among the poor. This again is no different from the fundamental spirit in which I myself have advocated universal suffrage.[27]

To those who opposed universal suffrage as an 'alien ideology', such as Tōyama who wished to restrict the franchise to heads of families, he defended it in terms of Emperor Meiji's Charter Oath and equated 'Kantian individualism' with the 'inner light' of Yōmeigaku. He also represented himself as following in Saigō's footsteps—describing him as a man of 'passionate sincerity' whose political strategy lay in 'capturing and guiding the popular mind.'

Another factor making for traditionalism was the continued influence of his spiritual guide, Kaneko, who figures in an often repeated anecdote about Nakano's early days in the Diet, bearing on his financial problems. These included the support of his numerous dependents (which included four sons by 1922) and the deficits regularly run by the *Tōhō Jiron* after the 1920 slump, while political expenses were as always heavy.

When someone therefore proposed in Kaneko's presence that an effort might be made to raise money to help Nakano, Kaneko retorted forcefully that no Diet member had ever been known to starve—they were too intent on making their own fortunes! If in contrast, Nakano were to faint during his maiden speech and this were to be found to be due to hunger, it would so resound to his credit that he would be well cared for subsequently, as well as distinguishing Japan in the eyes of the whole world. Kaneko closed by asserting that, throughout history, all men of dedication had been prepared to face such hardships.

Influences of this kind led Nakano to persist for some time in the role of lone and dedicated 'patriot' (*shishi*), devoted more to forceful crusading than to the formulation of precise policies.

Another example of Kaneko's influence was a students' welfare project which Nakano initiated about this time and maintained for the rest of his life. He and his dependents were then living in a house at Harajuku owned by his Mitsui backer, Takagi, but the house was extended to accommodate about five students at a time, whose fees and other needs he met from income derived from lecture fees (averaging ¥40–50). This centre was named the Yūkōkyo (after Nakano's constituency organisation) and was no doubt largely inspired by the example of Kaneko's Shintōsha Academy at Dairen.

The students helped Nakano in various ways, including election campaigning and in defending the house against hostile political thugs, as well as providing him later on with some political organisers. The two chief examples are Hasegawa Shun and Nagata Masayoshi, who respectively directed Nakano's publicity and his Youth Corps from the later 1930s. He also lectured to them on Confucian texts such as the 'Great Learning', though in the Diet he could oppose a conservative proposal for the state promotion of classical Chinese learning to combat the 'new thought' which, he argued, could only be handled on the basis of 'economic and scientific studies'.[28] He was only interested in using traditional thought in the cause of protest and condemned its use in the interests of the established order (*taigimeibun-shugi* or the principle of perceiving one's duty in terms of one's station in life).

Another factor which tended to prolong his traditionalist posture was the swift decay of the extra party radical movement which, contrary to his earlier hopes, failed to generate much momentum. As early as September 1920 he expressed disappointment that the popular movement now seemed to have been a 'fashionable trend stemming from passing impulse'. He added that, for his part, he could support neither 'despotic' nor 'inflammatory' politicians. Universal suffrage would not automatically solve everything, as 'even those without the vote can influence the vote, while the vote without intelligence is useless'. With the distrust of westernised intelligentsia which he never lost, he said, 'We certainly do not need the present-day intelligentsia who merely add a "smell of butter" [Western flavour] to empty discussion aloof from real life.' His solution was the patient development of a broad based small man's party, financed by its members' contributions rather than by big business[29]—a hope to which he constantly returned whenever the situation seemed favourable.

Since the 'reconstruction' movement on the home front now seemed to be lagging, Nakano preferred for the time to concentrate on foreign policy issues, especially, no doubt, as he had derived so much impetus from the Peace Conference. The government's weakest point in this area was the Russian question on which he waged a vigorous campaign for some years. This involved some risk in his own constituency, where the Kokuryūkai element was first and foremost anti-Russian, though his stand also served to form connections with businessmen interested in trade with the Soviet Union, such as Matsukata Kōjirō of the Kawasaki Shipbuilding Company, who later accompanied him on a visit to Siberia.

Nakano's maiden speech in July 1920 was devoted to this question and more particularly to the recent massacre at Nikolaevsk of some hundreds of Japanese by partisan irregulars. He certainly showed remarkable courage in confronting the anti-Russian frenzy which followed this incident and attempting to divert it against the government. Supporting a motion by both opposition parties for a committee of enquiry, he took the opportunity to survey the whole question. In doing so he fired the opening shot of what became a prolonged feud against War Minister Tanaka Giichi, who was in the process of becoming the chief representative of the Chōshū clique. Nakano concentrated on denouncing the independence of General Staff action,[30] which in a current article he claimed made the 'military clique' a 'second cabinet'.

Early next year he moved that the government 'clarify its policy of non-intervention in Russia [to which it claimed to be moving] and establish a basis for mutually beneficial trade relations'. In his speech he discounted the common fear that contact with the Soviet Union would open Japan to subversive influences. He described socialism as a stereoscopic 'panorama' with external appeal but lacking depth. Contact with it would expose the hollowness of its advocates' claims—not win converts.[31]

He made the same point in commenting on the murder of a socialist by the Sekka Bōshidan (Anti-Bolshevik Corps), recommending the cool analysis of socialism as a better antidote to it than "Blackshirt-style violence'—a noteworthy contrast with the more favourable picture of fascism he formed much later. In any case, his support for friendly relations with the Soviet Union never implied any favour for socialism, which he always rejected and against which he framed more systematic arguments as his thought developed.

But on the diplomatic level he believed that an understanding with the Soviet Union would strengthen Japan's position in dealing with the Western powers and in this Diet speech he recalled, as he often did, how cooperation with Russia had stood Japan is good stead before the First World War in blocking British plans to construct a railway competing with the South Manchurian Railway.

As a corollary to this stand, Nakano naturally opposed the agreements reached at the Washington Conference in the same year which, to him, extended the Versailles system by integrating East Asia into an Anglo–American dominated framework. He therefore moved a resolution in the Diet in February 1922 that: 'The government has been remiss in seeking the nation's understanding of developments at the Washington Conference.'[32] He questioned the foreign minister's assurance that the world was now in an age of 'international accord' and claimed instead that the United States was using the popular desire for disarmament as a bait to open up East Asia to its own exploitation without any reciprocal opening of its own preserve in Latin America. Elsewhere he argued that Britain had allowed the Washington agreements to supersede the Anglo–Japanese Alliance because Japan's foolish clash with the Soviet Union had relieved the British of any fears of Russian pressure on their own Asian possessions.

Yet again, in 1923, he moved for the recognition of the Soviet Union, at the same time advocating the admission of the wartime enemy states to the League of Nations as a further counter to Anglo–American dominance. He painted an optimistic picture of the possibilities of trade and investment in the Soviet Union under the New Economic Policy, which in turn had also demonstrated the limitations of socialism. Broad world policies of this kind, he argued, would cure Japan's intellectual narrowness, bred of too much isolation.[33]

Nakano's extra-Diet activities in this area included public speaking on the Russian question in the company of well-known socialists, and the publicising of a visit by Antonov, representative of the Far Eastern Republic buffer state, who had visited Japan to explore the possibilities of Japanese investment and a Sino–Soviet–Japanese bloc directed against the Western powers. Another related episode was a visit to Korea and Manchuria in late 1920 on which Nakano produced the series 'Reflected in the Mirror of Manchuria and Korea' (*Mansen no Kagami ni utsushite*) for the *Kokumin Shimbun*, later also published in book form. This experience led to another Diet motion by him for a committee of enquiry on Korea, with a recommendation to extend the full provisions of the Constitution to that territory—which otherwise might produce an equivalent of the Irish Sinn Fein.[34]

Meanwhile Nakano did his best to extend his political alliances while retaining the maximum degree of independence. In early 1921 he joined in the formation of the Independents' (*Mushozoku*) Club which in turn, late the following year, amalgamated with the Kokumintō and other elements to form the Renovation (*Kakushin*) Club.

This body partly represented a last bid by elements of the new generation to achieve an alternative political style contrasting with that of the major parties, having no formal head or party-type organisation. Its inaugural manifesto stated that the club aimed to free the political process from the vices of the old style parties, which could no longer satisfy the popular mind of the postwar era. Its foreign policy favoured a program of economic rather than territorial expansion (*Sangyō Rikkoku saku*)—as long advocated by Inukai.

Members included Nakano's former patron in the *Asahi*, Yugeta Seiichi, as well as a number of members who later achieved prominence, but although it functioned as a modest third force in the Diet, it hardly represented a serious alternative or challenge to the two major parties. Nagai with his usual realism called on all its members to join the Kenseikai, as only the major parties could wield much influence, but Nakano as always was more reluctant to come to terms with current power structures and preferred to gamble on the prospects of change. Inukai's lieutenant and Nakano's old friend Kojima admits having promoted the formation of the Club to keep Inukai's Diet following above the minimum required for a negotiating body (*kōshō dantai*) i.e. a group entitled to proportional representation in Diet committees. But he describes it as a 'motley lot' and his voluminous biography dismisses it in a few lines as 'transitional'.[35]

A roughly parallel body outside the Diet in which Nakano then participated was the Yūshinsha (Renewal Society) which included his lifelong friend Kazami and Professor Mitsukawa of the former Rōsōkai. Though having its headquarters in the *Tōhō Jiron's* premises like the earlier Tōhōkai, its activities were more political and concentrated especially on the Russian question. Its manifesto, reflecting current pessimism regarding the prospects of mass action, tended to be elitist, saying: 'If the nation is not yet truly awakened, choice spirits must band together from within it and, while tackling contemporary problems, seek for fellow-thinkers in all quarters.[36]

For a number of years from about this time—in fact until he formed his own political organisation—Nakano was too preoccupied with political action to keep up regular journalistic work. Another factor which reduced occasions for writing was the Kanto Earthquake of 1923, in which both the *Tōhō Jiron* and Miyake's *Nihon oyobi Nihonjin* lost their premises. The two of them combined to bring out a new journal called *Gakan* which also bore its title romanised as 'Gakwan', as well as sometimes an English translation reading 'My Views' or 'Our Views'. Miyake was usually named as proprietor or chief editor and the first issue (October 1923) bore a statement to the effect that his earlier *Nihonjin*, being chiefly concerned with Japan's role in the 'Eastern hemisphere', had been too narrowly conceived for the new world situation.

Nakano held the post of manager but the expression of his views in the journal was restricted by Miyake's conservative associates who disapproved of the stands of both of them on the Russian question. Nakano therefore for many years wrote for it only sporadically and its contents tended to be more literary than political. His youngest brother, Hideto, who was of an artistic bent, often contributed pieces.

From 1924, in any case, Nakano was chiefly occupied with the domestic political situation, where the campaign for manhood suffrage was coming to a head with the combination of most elements of the three main political groups against Kiyoura's 'Peers' Cabinet'. This alliance was termed the 'Second Movement to Defend the Constitution', the chief intermediary in forming it being General Miura, who had resigned from the Privy Council for this purpose. The only substantial opposition came from the Seiyūkai breakaways in the Seiyūhontō under Tokonami Takejirō, who hoped that the cabinet's very weakness might make it profitable to support.

The three-party alliance aroused none of the popular involvement which had been called forth in the Taishō Crisis and the immediate postwar suffrage movement, and its early phase had been criticised for this reason by Nakano, who wrote: 'For Japan as it is today, a mass movement is essential to overcome the status quo in the anti-status quo movement itself, to renovate the Renovation Club and to give true leadership to the nation'. But the overwhelming success of the alliance in the election of May 1924 proved decisive so far as the ruling Establishment was concerned.

In this election, however, Nakano was returned only with the greatest difficulty, gaining 2784 votes to the 2758 won by his rival Miyagawa, who now had Seiyūkai connections. Among reasons given for the narrow margin are the hostility of the Kokuryūkai to Nakano's position on the Russian question, Nakano's relative neglect of his constituents' material interests in favour of ideological issues and the shift of Kakushin Club elements towards the Seiyūkai, with which the club later amalgamated. But a more basic reason was the system of single-member constituencies introduced by the Hara government, which made electoral success more difficult for smaller parties and independents.

Nakano was therefore compelled to make a realistic assessment of his chances of future success in practical politics, which were now clearly slender without support from the resources of one or other of the two major parties. Besides, even when he was in possession of a Diet seat, none of the motions he had put with only minority backing had been successful. Of the two major parties, the Kenseikai was much the more congenial in view of the relative strength of its progressive 'party men's' wing centred on Adachi Kenzō (i.e. professional politicians as distinguished from members of career bureaucrat background), which included Nagai and Miki. These were both Waseda graduates and facilitated Nakano's entry into the party. His move is also explained as influenced by the reasonable hope of an ultimate ministerial post and his wife is described as especially pleased with this prospect[38] which, on the family level, would have demonstrated to her mother that Nakano was a good match after all.

In a letter to Inukai severing his connection with the Kakushin Club, Nakano made the point that only the two major parties had any real hope of wielding effective power, while the club had itself by now lost any distinctive character—the only possibility for a new political style lying in the still remote prospect of a social–democratic type party.

From this time on Nakano's relations with Inukai remained poor until the latter's death. Early in 1925 he attacked Inukai over various issues on the occasion of his failure to meet Sun Yat-sen during a visit to Japan.[39] Then, when the club finally merged with the Seiyūkai, now headed by General Tanaka, the two men were ranged on opposite sides in a bitter political struggle.

Adjustment to party politics

Within the Kenseikai and its successor the Minseitō, Nakano remained throughout fully identified with Adachi's faction. Unlike the case of the Seiyūkai, where 'party men' formed factions around career bureaucrat leaders, such men in this party formed a distinct group around Adachi—its general features being described as the absence of Imperial University graduates, a commitment to the postwar 'reconstruction' theme and a special concern with Chinese questions, as well as an association with elements which later formed part of the extreme Right[40]—in Nakano's case, for instance, Kita Ikki and Araki Sadao, with whom he retained links from the earlier Tōhōkai days.

Adachi himself originated from Kumamoto and in his youth had been active in the local right wing party, the Kokkentō (National Rights Party), then becoming an adventurer in Korea, where he played a leading part in the coup which resulted in Queen Min's murder. Later he became a Diet member in the pro-government Chūō Club and subsequently the Dōshikai, in which he earned the soubriquet 'god of elections' for his able role in the notorious election held under the Ōkuma Cabinet in 1915.

Despite this background, such a consistent, if conservatively inclined, liberal as Ogata writes of him with high praise, to the effect that 'he performed his duties faithfully as the manager of a great party, his character being of a peerless integrity which would never betray a trust'. Certainly in 1924 he rendered good service in marshalling the forces that achieved the best, if modest, fruits of 'Taishō democracy'. He also introduced the system of medium-sized multi-member constituencies which since prevailed at most times and later, in 1931, took the lead in pushing the first trade union legislation through the Lower House, though it was blocked in the Peers through the efforts of Baron Dan of Mitsui.

After joining the Kenseikai under Adachi's patronage, Nakano's image steadily evolved towards that of a regular party politician, giving high priority to his constituents' interests on the usual pork-barrel lines and defending party policies even when these were not wholly congenial. Despite his earlier criticism of the established parties, he now described the achievements of Katō Kōmei's coalition cabinet—notably manhood suffrage and the recognition of the Soviet Union—as a 'victory for popular initiative over slavery at home and the Anglo–American power monopoly abroad'.[41] The party, in return, utilised his already recognised talent for publicity by soon appointing him head of its Propaganda Department.

Within the range allowed by the framework of party politics he was still distinguished by a special taste for aggressive debate, as well as retaining something of the rugged warrior image—an example of this being his gift of a sword in 1925 to Ogata, who had been injured in an attack on *Asahi* staff by the Anti-Bolshevik Corps.[42] But the attenuation of his earlier attitudes is indicated by a period of cooler relations with Tōyama who, as mentioned, had opposed manhood suffrage. Nakano is said to have now habitually avoided his company in Tokyo ostensibly because he did not wish to give the impression of flattering him for his own ends or to be restricted by relations with him.

Nakano now also criticised the older school of Pan-Asianists for their 'religious-type faith' in Asian cultural values and their racial hatred for all white nations, with a special distaste for collaboration with the Soviet Union. This attitude he contrasted with Sun Yat-sen's freedom from racism and his readiness to make common cause with ostracised white nations against the dominant group. Again, whereas Rabindranath Tagore, the leading international exponent of traditional Asian culture, had been welcomed in Japan by Tōyama's group, Sun's following in China had properly condemned Tagore for trying once more to lull to sleep those who had once been awakened to the need for scientific thought and industrialisation.[43]

Nakano's most obvious problem in adjusting to his party's line was presented by Foreign Minister Shidehara's diplomacy which was based on acceptance of the Washington Pact order and committed to the 'open door in East Asia'. In guarded criticism of Shidehara, Nakano described his neutralism on Chinese questions as too negative and urged a more positive neutrality in the direction of 'Far Eastern Monroeism', meaning a concomitant resistance to intervention in the region by outside powers.[44]

One issue on which Nakano under the Katō cabinet found himself much in the minority was that of the Peace Preservation Law. In consolidating various earlier measures for the suppression of radical thought, this for the first time made ideological commitment itself a grave offence if opposed to the existing form of government or to the system of private property. Nakano was one of a minority group of members from various parties who vainly campaigned against its passage. Although he was free of any leaning towards socialism and had no wish to challenge the form of the Constitution, he was in some degree threatened by a law of this kind to the extent that he advocated certain political reforms, as well as improved relations with the Soviet Union.

He persisted in this latter cause, however, and in late 1925 visited Siberia, Manchuria and North China, attended by Shintō Kazuma, son of the recently deceased Genyōsha leader Shintō Kiheita. Shintō was then a student at Waseda but later became Nakano's secretary and ultimately succeeded to his electoral base.

They were accompanied to Siberia by Matsukata of the Kawasaki Shipbuilding Company and other businessmen, then travelled to Peking, where Nakano was welcomed by his former fellow-student Lin Ch'ang-min, now Chairman of the Constitutional Drafting Committee. After making a speech to Lin's colleagues advocating a customs union of China and Japan on China's approaching recovery of tariff autonomy, he travelled with Shintō to Paotow, Inner Mongolia, to meet the warlord then dominant in North China, the 'Christian General', Feng Yü-hsiang. According to Nakano's own account,[45] he found Feng markedly favourable to socialism, which Nakano then attacked on the grounds that a society suppressing individualism eliminates all free initiative and falls into bureaucratic regimentation. To Feng's demand for the relinquishment of Japan's rights in Manchuria, he replied that Feng's own socialist thinking should value rights derived from use more highly than a mere claim to ownership. He felt some disquiet about the degree of Russian influence in Feng's regime as, contrary to his usual rather facile hopes, such influence seemed, when seen in this setting, likely to clash more directly with Japanese interests than with those of the Western Powers. Whether his account of the interview is quite accurate or not, the views he expresses in it do reflect concerns which tended to occupy Nakano's mind in the ensuing period.

The feud with Tanaka

The inter-party mud slinging so prevalent in this period, naturally gave Nakano plenty of scope to exercise his combative talents and in the process become better known. In March 1926 he began a series of intense attacks on General Tanaka, who now led the Seiyūkai in opposition to Wakatsuki's Kenseikai cabinet. He first accused Tanaka of having, while War Minister during the Siberian Intervention, misappropriated a vast sum of secret service funds and used this both for private purposes and for securing his presidency of the Seiyūkai.

Various allegations on this question were already circulating from Satsuma-clique quarters, partly because the Seiyūhontō leader Tokonami (originating from Satsuma) hoped to supplant Tanaka as the next in line for prime minister and partly because the Satsuma clique in the General Staff hoped to use the issue to combat Chōshū domination in army circles. Finally, a former army accountant under Tanaka when War Minister laid formal charges at the Procurator-General's Office against him and his vice-minister at the time for having treated as their own property at least ¥8 000 000 in bonds held in the ministry's safe.

On the same day Nakano brought the matter before the Diet in the form of an urgency motion to the effect that since Tanaka as a Peer could not be examined by a Lower House committee of enquiry, such a committee be formed to examine Hatoyama Ichirō and others privy to Tanaka's appointment as Seiyūkai president. Nakano estimated the funds not accounted for as amounting to ¥24 000 000.

The Seiyūkai soon counter attacked with a resolution calling for Nakano's resignation from the Diet for trying to discredit the army in the interests of communist revolution. They cited alleged witnesses in Manchuria and supposed Vladivostok newspaper reports in claiming that Nakano had been financed for this purpose on his recent visit to Siberia. Although a committee of enquiry found that these accusations lacked any substance, the struggle continued in various forms. Outside the Diet, Nakano was attacked in publications of obscure provenance (*kaibunsho*) of which at least one survives, produced by a 'League for the Breaking of Diplomatic Relations with Russia', recounting supposed details of his activities as a communist agent identified as 'Tovarich [Comrade] 818'. He also had to be assigned special guards to protect him from violence in the Diet itself, while he was threatened at home and at public meetings by Seiyūkai thugs (*sōshi*). In meeting such threats he was assisted by his student boarders, as well as by his own party's *sōshi* and other stalwarts. He also publicised his views in book form as a 'Collection of Articles on Russia and China Policies' (*Tai Roshi Ronsakushū*) (1926).

In view of the implications of this scandal for the army as a whole, the government's own War Minister, General Ugaki Kazushige, protested to Wakatsuki, who assured both him and the Diet that the attack had been made on the initiative of certain party members only and had not been officially sanctioned by the party. This seems likely enough, in view of the usual divergencies among factions, as well as Wakatsuki's unwillingness at all times to agree to all-out confrontations. The only ultimate consequence of this contest was the expulsion of a Seiyūkai Diet member who was found to have bribed two Seiyūhontō members.

For a time in mid-1926 Nakano was out of action owing to surgical treatment involving the loss of a leg. He had been slightly lame ever since the judo accident suffered in his early youth, which had led to several operations and his rejection for military service. He was now persuaded to undergo corrective surgery but the operation was followed by pain so intense that he finally asked for the leg to be amputated. When the leg was opened up the surgeon was shocked at the deterioration that had set in and agreed that there was no alternative but to amputate. This was some consolation to Nakano, who was rather ashamed of not having shown as much stoicism as he would have liked. He is said to have spoken of resolving to behave less hot headedly in the future. His son comments that at least he was no longer able to take any part in Diet brawls, in which he had taken some pride in handling himself well.

The preceding phase of inter-party recrimination was suspended at the beginning of 1927 by a truce concluded between Wakatsuki, Tanaka and Tokonami, ostensibly as a token of respect for the new Emperor whose reign had just begun.

Adachi and Finance Minister Hamaguchi Osachi were angered at this decision, as they were confident of success if Wakatsuki had challenged the opposition to an election—the first under manhood suffrage, which the Kenseikai had done most to achieve. Wakatsuki's account pleads his financial limitations in defence of this decision[46] but the younger party men were deeply disappointed and one of Adachi's proteges, Miki Bukichi, resigned his post of finance ministry councillor in protest.

As a member of the same faction, he persuaded Nakano to take over this position. At first Nakano was reluctant to accept it, telling Miki that his ambition lay in 'broad national politics' while financial matters were the province of mere *kanjō bugyō* (rather despised financial officers under the feudal order) with which he would prefer not to be identified. Miki argued in reply that no future statesman could dispense with a knowledge of economic matters and Nakano agreed to accept the post. This marked a further stage in his evolution away from concentration on ideological crusading to a greater concern with specialised administrative problems—a development which left its mark even when he later returned to more extremist political activity. Shibata says that from about this time Nakano's intellectual development was so marked that on his yearly visits to Fukuoka his old associates there felt that he was growing steadily more remote from them[47].

He only held this particular post for a couple of months owing to the cabinet's fall in the wake of the 'Shōwa Financial Crisis' (named for the new Emperor's reign title) which led to the collapse of the smaller banking sector. As the Diet was not in session, the cabinet proposed to deal with the matter by emergency ordinance, requiring the consent of the Privy Council. In the Council, however, the influential member Itō Miyoji concentrated on condemning the conciliatory Shidehara line in China, which he claimed disregarded the Kuomintang alliance with the communists and the damage suffered by Japanese interests in incidents at Nanking and Hankow. His stand led to the blocking of the government's financial proposals as well, upon which Wakatsuki resigned as prime minister and was succeeded by Tanaka.

Nakano's first action against the Tanaka cabinet was to submit a motion—pressed by all the younger party men—censuring the Privy Council for infringing the principles of constitutional government in that, on the one hand, it had defied the cabinet which was responsible to the people and, on the other, had advised the Emperor on a matter (diplomacy) which he had not first submitted to it. Nakano attacked Itō in the bitterest terms, likening him to the proverbial traitors and court plotters of Sung Dynasty China, Ch'in Kuai and Wang Lun:

> 'Cut down Ch'in Kuai! Cut down Wang Lun!'—this was the cry of patriots in that age. We, too, are convinced that it is the nation's inescapable resolve today to have Itō's head, wielding the redoubtable sword of public opinion![48]

The motion of censure was carried—an event unique in the Diet's history. But the veteran liberal Ozaki Yukio remarked that the former government should at least have sought the Emperor's dismissal of the offending councillors and he cautioned the young sponsors of the motion against making too many enemies if they hoped to gain responsible posts in the future. Nakano, however, as usual paid little attention to such advice, as he showed when opportunities soon arose for making even more vitriolic attacks on Tanaka.

Before long, the new government began a revision of China policy by holding an Eastern Regions Conference, organised by the energetic Vice-Minister of Foreign Affairs, Mori Kaku, who had a background of Mitsui interests in China and had been associated with the Tōhōkai. The conference was attended by representatives of all relevant administrative, diplomatic and armed service agencies and decided that if the hitherto cooperative Manchurian warlord Chang Tso-lin was driven from North China by the Kuomintang, Japan would assume a more direct control of Manchurian affairs. Some concern was caused abroad by announcements that the Japanese army would intervene if the Chinese failed to keep order, but further moves were suspended as the split between Chiang Kai-shek and the communists developed. A curious by-product of this conference was the creation of the legend that it had formulated a 'Tanaka Memorial' as a blueprint for world conquest, sometimes called 'Japan's *Mein Kampf*'.

In May 1928, however, Chiang pressed on with the northern campaign and as his forces approached Tsinan the Japanese government at Mori's insistence despatched troops there to protect Japanese interests, leading to armed clashes. A statement was then issued on Japan's preparedness to enforce order in Manchuria and the Kwantung army headquarters was moved to Mukden. But even when Chang was finally driven from Peking, Tanaka made no further move because of United States warnings. Army elements on the spot therefore decided to eliminate Chang, which they did by blowing up his train, though the true nature of the incident long remained obscure. While Tanaka announced that any army personnel implicated in the incident would be punished, Japanese representatives on the spot warned Chang's son and successor Hsüeh-liang against unification with China, though no action was taken when he soon afterwards took this step.

A little later, in a speech at Fukuoka with a markedly anti-traditionalist slant, entitled 'The Revision of China Policies', Nakano surveyed Chang's career which, up to a point, resembled that of many successful bandits in Chinese history who had attained great political power and even the throne—which obsequious scholars would then explain as due to their virtue, in accordance with the Confucian doctrine of the Mandate of Heaven. But Chang, once in possession of Peking, had failed to meet the novel challenges posed by the 'moralistic United States', 'gentlemanly but crafty Britain' and the 'organisation of international self-righteousness' called the League of Nations, as well as the Soviet Union and the awakening people of China. Nakano went on to attack Tanaka for futile opposition to this awakening.[49]

Later in the year he published a pamphlet entitled 'The Fiasco of Tanaka Diplomacy' (*Tanaka Gaikō no Sampai*) and in the Diet Budget Committee session the following January he launched a marathon attack on Tanaka spread over three day sessions, which is described as having had no parallel in the Diet's history.

Although this attack is usually represented as aimed against militarism and expansionism as such, in strange contrast with Nakano's later fervent support for the authors of the Manchurian Incident, he explicitly denied that he intended to pass judgement on Chang's murder itself, but only on the context of government policies in which it occurred.[50] This is very different from his earlier wholesale attacks on the military clique in Terauchi's time, though even then he was most concerned with clan dominance. He now more carefully narrowed the object of his attack to the cabinet itself in an effort to overthrow it—a result to which he ultimately contributed.

Far from condemning the army, he dwelt on the embarrassing position in which the Kwantung army was placed by Tanaka's declaration on Japan's responsibility for keeping order, followed by his backing down at the United States reaction. He stressed the state of crisis prevailing in Manchuria in a way which, though now meant to embarrass the government, could also later lend itself to justifying more drastic action.

When Nakano pursued Tanaka's responsibility for such incidents as the handover to Chinese guards, at their request, of the stretch of railway where the bombing took place, and the warning to Chang Hsüeh-liang not to unite with Nanking, Tanaka weakly blamed his agents on the spot, saying that myriads of prime ministers would not suffice to supervise such matters directly. Later, when Nakano questioned why the government now accepted Manchuria's unification with China and had opened tariff negotiations with Nanking despite the latter's refusal to reconsider its abrogation of the Treaty of Commerce, Tanaka claimed that Nanking's attitude had softened in spirit but was unable to demonstrate this. Nakano did define his own position as favouring Chinese unification but urged realism regarding Japan's interests. Tanaka was in the end so cornered that he refused all comment 'in the national interest' and Nakano called for his resignation in the words:

> Which is the more important—Tanaka Giichi's personal position or the dignity of the State and the honour of the Imperial Forces? Cannot you forego your position for the sake of our country?[51]

According to Adachi, Nakano's attack did not represent any official party decision, it being agreed to let him have a free hand, as he seemed to possess information of which the source was not clear. This would seem to refer to contact with the 'young officer' elements, of which more signs emerge later and which would explain Nakano's care not to attack the army as such.

He was, however, still in a dilemma regarding Chinese policy. Although the Shidehara line was still favoured by his party and he and Nagai reaffirmed support for it on Nanking's abrogation of the Treaty of Commerce, it had never been very congenial to him and had not secured Japan's position in China. But neither could he accept the rival party's 'positive policy' which in any case had clearly misfired. As he wrote afterwards, it had only hardened China's stand and shown that the traditional imperialist methods of military-political intervention would no longer work—these must be replaced by more sophisticated socio-economic pressures. 'The mere schemes of a military clique are out of date'.[52] He had moved some distance towards the position where he could welcome the 'breakthrough' by the young officers in the Manchurian Incident a couple of years later.

Most of the ultranationalists, of course, did not appreciate his fine distinction between Tanaka and the army. The 'Pure Japanist' periodical *Nippon*, associated with Baron Hiranuma and Kita Ikki's brother Reikichi, described him as 'a Japanese anti-Japanist collaborating with the Chinese anti-Japanists', and threats of violence from the right as well as by Seiyūkai *sōshi* recurred. As additional insurance, he is said by one admittedly doubtful source to have obtained through Kita Ikki the help of an influential right wing extremist of Fukuoka origin, Terada Inejirō, who in that year joined in forming the Nippon Kokumintō and for some time served as Nakano's 'bodyguard'.[53] In any case, from this time Nakano tended to develop contacts not only with the 'renovationist' elements in the army but with the growing right wing as well.

The Minseitō

Before this last phase of Nakano's campaign against Tanaka, he had taken a leading part in forming a new party, the Rikken Minseitō (Constitutional Popular Government Party) by the amalgamation of the Kenseikai with the Seiyūhontō. Tokonami had agreed to this merger following his failure to succeed Wakatsuki as prime minister, but the move provided an opportunity for the Kenseikai 'party men's' wing to introduce a platform reflecting their ideas on national reconstruction. This included not only Diet-centred politics and broad-based diplomacy aimed at securing the resources needed for Japan's economic development, but also state regulation of production and distribution. Nakano and Nagai (now classed among Adachi's four chief supporters) both became party directors, with Nakano also as campaign manager. In this capacity he actively opened branches throughout the country in pursuit of his hopes for a mass-based party. He and his associates also energetically supported progressive extra-Diet groups such as the Waseda-based Daiisen Dōmei (Frontline League).

Nakano, in 1928, for a time became president of the *Kyūshū Nippō* newspaper, the Genyōsha organ originally named the *Fukuryō Shimpō*, and retained control of it until it was taken over by *Yomiuri* in 1940. This doubtless helped him consolidate his local support and in the election of 1928 he won the largest number of votes in the constituency. On this occasion, his constituency organisation was renamed the Seigōkai.

The Minseitō president was Hamaguchi, who was assured of finance from Mitsubishi sources but was essentially associated with the senior career bureaucrat wing of the party. Most of these, rather than feeling any strong commitment to the party platform, had merely recognised its appeal to the expanded electorate.[54] The power balance in the party was demonstrated when Hamaguchi succeeded Tanaka as prime minister on the latter's resignation in the wake of the Chang Incident, as the new cabinet was dominated by the bureacratic wing and its connections. Nakano later wrote of the party's principles as having been lost on its attaining power since, in the party as a whole, there persisted an awe of professional bureaucratic authority because most party members had not had much opportunity to acquire adequate administrative expertise.[55] Such a comment also indicates the new importance he had come to place on this type of qualification for office, in opposition to bureaucrats with more specialised experience following recruitment through the examination system.

While Adachi was Home Minister, such key posts as foreign and finance ministers went to non-party men, Shidehara and Inoue Junnosuke respectively. In contrast with the party plank of state economic regulation, Inoue was a classic *laissez faire* liberal, perpetuating the Kenseikai 'negative economic policy' of frugality and retrenchment and committed to the ill-timed return to the gold standard. The Shidehara diplomatic line would later also prove ready to accept the perpetuation of naval limitation under the London Naval Treaty.

As compensation for the domination of cabinet posts by the bureaucratic wing, the Adachi faction were given seven of the twelve vice-ministerial posts. Nakano was finally placed as Vice-Minister of Communications—with some difficulty because, while his talents for publicity and debate were appreciated, his suitability for administrative office was in some doubt. Nakano himself doubted his suitability for this particular post but was at least on good terms with the minister, Koizumi Matajirō, a veteran campaigner for universal suffrage and party man. Nakano certainly showed his usual energy in using the opportunities arising from the position.

One of his first acts was, in conjunction with the permanent Vice-Minister, to prevent a retrenchment in the ministry's wage budget by having Koizumi threaten to resign. This earned Nakano popularity among the employees, which subsequently led to his obtaining office in one of their trade unions.

He also used the position to protect the interests of his constituents in the prevailing pork-barrel style; he suggested to the Kyushu Electricity Association that they apply for the establishment of a regional testing laboratory—apparently a profitable undertaking, which was duly approved before those for other areas outside the Kanto and Kansai regions.[56]

His post also enabled him to recruit his close friend since Waseda days, Kazami Akira, as a strong new member of Adachi's faction in the Diet. Kazami was only now switching his interests from progressive journalism to politics and Nakano accompanied him on speaking tours in his constituency in the Mito region, as well as setting up post offices to assist him. Kazami was accordingly elected for the Minseitō in 1930 and, as will be seen, proved an active ally. He also became the chief organiser for the revived Tōkōhai centred on *Gakan* staff—the nucleus of Nakano's later party—which now extended its interests to Indian affairs through contacts with Ras Bihari Bose, a political refugee whom Tōyama had earlier saved from extradition.

Nakano's chief official undertaking during the eighteen months in his post was to develop a plan for reorganising the communications services. This is usually described as the 'Telegraph and Telephone Private Management Plan' (*Denshin Denwa Mineian*), though in a later article[57] Nakano explains that it amounted to the formation of a joint private and public company to carry out the development and maintenance of telecommunications facilities, drawing capital from private sources but subject to government legislation and control, the actual operation of services remaining in government hands. The plan, he claims, would have financed a great expansion of services at less cost to subscribers.

Departmental staff worked round the clock for months to carry out detailed research for the plan, which was attacked from both bureaucratic and socialist quarters. To the former, Nakano replied that the plan was in accordance with the Minseitō platform and that projects of this kind would help to restore the economy (which was languishing from the world depression and the return to the gold standard). To the socialists, he replied that he hoped to extend the state's functions to the mobilisation of private capital, in contrast with communism where everything would be state owned and controlled—leading to total bureaucratisation. The government needed ultimate control over the economy, but not ownership or direct management.

Although this approach was consistent with Nakano's usual mistrust of bureaucracy and socialism, he had recently been given a more concrete alternative by his reading of the British Fabian socialist, G.D.H. Cole, particularly *The Next Ten Years in British Social and Economic Policy* (1929). He had been introduced to Cole's work by his friend Professor Sugimori of Waseda and had applied his ideas in the telecommunications plan.

This particular book is represented by Cole in his Introduction as marking a turning-point in his thought away from utopian and doctrinaire socialism towards a more pragmatic approach to social problems. He advocates the rationalisation of industry but denies that any one model for this would be universally applicable and argues that a healthy society should be as 'self-acting' as possible (a point made long before by Nakano in criticising the administration of Korea). State power should be used, not for nationalisation and direct management by 'top-heavy bureaucracy' (a phrase adopted by Nakano with the English word 'top-heavy' transliterated) but for the 'control and direction of the economic life of the community' by some such means as overall supervision by an Economic General Staff backed by a Board of National Investment controlling all capital in the hands of public authorities, as well as funds to be raised by national investment bonds. By this means the State could favour enterprises which both showed promise of success and were likely to benefit the community most.

Given Nakano's ideological biases and the current demand for alternatives to classic liberalism and doctrinaire socialism, it was natural enough that he favoured this kind of program from this time on. His telecommunications plan was, however, frustrated as a result of Hamaguchi's wounding in November 1930 by a patriotic extremist in protest against the London Naval Treaty. Shidehara became acting prime minister and for the moment tried to avoid all controversial measures. Nakano's scheme was therefore suspended on the eve of its proposed implementation and, after bursting into the cabinet room and arguing heatedly with Finance Minister Inoue, he resigned his post.

This became the central turning point in his political life, as it marked the limit of his adaptation to a career pattern within the established order and the beginning of a steadily intensifying campaign for the recasting of national policies and institutions. He explains his resignation partly as a protest against the possibility that, in the event of a change in cabinets, the Seiyūkai might reap the credit for the research he had directed. He also wished to demonstrate a sense of responsibility for such a major effort and felt that he would now do better by concentrating on preparing the party for future electoral struggles. This suggests a conviction that he was not at his best in the setting of intra-party compromise and that his interests would now be better served by preserving his political credibility with a view to devoting his main efforts to influencing or ultimately attaining top-level leadership. Certainly his subsequent activities followed such a course.

Breakaway

Soon afterwards Nakano wrote a letter to the ill Hamaguchi deploring the state of the government.[58] In it he complained about Shidehara's appointment merely on the grounds of his Court rank and expressed support for a resolution recently passed by a group of junior party members, including Kazami, urging that party business be placed under the control of an acting party president who should be guided by the general will of members. Nakano denied that he or Adachi had instigated this move in their own interests, though there is little room for doubt that the Adachi wing were now doing their best to extend their influence, while attempting to devise policies capable of meeting the increasingly distraught political situation.

A series of articles written by Nakano over the next few months was published in August 1931 under the title 'The Rebirth of Stagnating Japan' (*Chintai Nihon no Kōsei*) and indicates the direction of his thought. It mainly deals with the problems posed by the worldwide depression, through which international trade had become subject to extreme protectionism, with the formation of largely self-contained blocs. Nakano minimises his theoretical differences with Finance Minister Inoue but stresses the need to overcome both *laissez faire* liberalism and paternalism by replacing narrow commercialistic measures with a political consciousness capable of taking the long view of social needs. This would, for example, compensate for controls by offering incentives, while his own telecommunications plan had provided an object lesson in what might be done by way of experiment. In his customary role as champion of the masses, he describes the plight of the countryside as observed on a recent visit to the Mito area—Kazami's constituency—and warns:

When administrators discuss financial and economic policies, the thing they must not forget is the livelihood of the masses who form the cells of the national finance and economy. Nothing can be accomplished if, before orthodox financial and economic principles reveal their efficacy, the cells of the national life wither away.[59]

This must reflect Kazami's recent activities in financing the establishment of Tachibana Kōsaburō's rural academy, the Aikyōjuku, which soon produced the Blood Brotherhood agrarian terrorist group.

Included in this pamphlet is a piece entitled 'The Reorganisation of Relations with China', which marks a parallel shift away from Shidehara diplomacy. Reviewing past relations as well as his own experiences, Nakano proposes a more imaginative policy working towards an East Asian bloc in which the tropics would supply raw materials, supplemented also by China while, as that country's industrialisation also progressed, Japan would shift its emphasis to more advanced industrial fields—suggesting future thinking on the lines of coprosperity.

At this stage, Nakano's arguments still remained within the range of intra-party debate but certainly also reflected contact with the young officer element. It is elsewhere recorded that earlier in the year he had attended convivial gatherings arranged to allow frank discussion between representatives of the army 'national defence state' school of thought, including Colonel Nagata Tetsuzan, and members of the *Asahi* staff like Ogata, whose anti-militarist reporting had produced tensions with the armed forces.[60]

When the Manchurian Incident erupted in September 1931, soon followed by Britain's decision to leave the gold standard, Nakano visited a number of both military and foreign ministry officials to discover their reactions. The former group included Araki and looked to Adachi as the only cabinet member capable of meeting the situation effectively. In cabinet, he was the only civilian minister urging sympathy for the army's problems and at the same time advised reimposing the gold embargo, but Inoue rejected this step and concentrated on blaming the Zaibatsu for their currency speculations.

Next Nakano directly approached Wakatsuki, now restored to the prime ministership, urging resoluteness in Manchuria, since divisions among the Powers would rule out any intervention by them. He also consulted leading financiers including Ikeda Seihin, who was rising to predominance in the Mitsui combine. Since the formation of the Minseitō, Nakano's financial connections and backing had markedly widened, particularly in Mitsui circles, also including from this time Yamashita Kamesaburō, a Kobe shipping magnate, who gave him both support and advice on international trade problems. Nakano's contacts with Ikeda later led to widespread accusations that they had conspired to overthrow the cabinet, since Mitsui was believed to have profited enormously from its speculations when the next cabinet restored the gold embargo. Any such considerations, however, must have been secondary to Nakano's primary aim of advancing Adachi's political fortunes in alliance with the young officers and business interests.

In an article published in the *Asahi* in November,[61] he accused the Nanking Government of aggression in pressing into Manchuria, which had never been an integral part of China. He also attacked the policy usually advocated by Inukai (now leader of the Seiyūkai) of national advancement through economic development, on the grounds that a purely trading power without control of natural resources must inevitably decline like Athens or the Hanseatic League. He therefore urged that Japan integrate its economy with Manchuria, partly by the migration of Japanese labour, even if this were not as cheap as the local labour hitherto relied upon. In return, Japan would help the 'Free State of the Four Eastern Provinces' to build a 'multiracial Utopia', prospering through Japanese enterprise.

Nakano's swift alignment in favour of the Manchurian adventure, in contrast with his doubts about such methods in Tanaka's time, probably not only reflected his links with the young officers but also the role played by the Manchurian–Mongol Youth League (*Mammō Seinen Remmei*) which had originated under the influence of Kaneko (now dead) and was currently engaged in political manoeuvres coordinated with the army's operations. Kazami, who managed Kaneko's newspaper in Dairen for a time after his death, had been in Manchuria not long before the Incident erupted. Nakano's subsequent judgement of the Incident was that it had provided 'an opportunity for national resurgence in defiance of bureaucrats, politicians and the military clique'.[62] In this list he presumably included only representatives of these categories who were in power at the time.

Late in October Wakatsuki and Adachi discussed the possibility of stabilising the situation by setting up a coalition with the Seiyūkai, though several distinct sources describe Nakano as the main mover behind this plan. In any case, Wakatsuki authorised Adachi to sound out key political figures on the idea and both Prince Saionji, chief arbiter in cabinet formation, and Kuhara Fusanosuke, secretary-general of the Seiyūkai, were found in favour. Kuhara was confident that Inukai could be won over and would not 'press his own demands too stubbornly'. Adachi was, however, compelled to suspend these activities in mid-November to accompany the Emperor on grand manoeuvres in his native Kumamoto. He therefore briefed his faction leaders, now including Secretary-General Yamaji Jōichi and Party

Councillor Tomita Kōjirō, asking them to promote the idea discreetly in his absence. He describes Nakano, however, as having pressed it too openly.

Meanwhile Wakatsuki had been persuaded by Inoue and Shidehara, who could have had no place in the new regime, to drop the plan and Adachi was informed of this decision on his return. He nevertheless continued to contact Kuhara through Tomita and early in December these two reached a working agreement to the effect that both parties would cooperate in forming a coalition, that offices would be filled without discrimination as to party and that both would cooperate sincerely in framing new policies.[63] This agreement was publicly announced and Tomita tried to show a copy of it to Wakatsuki who, by his own account, refused even to look at it and called a cabinet meeting to suppress the move. Adachi was summoned last, with the aim of overawing him, but he refused either to attend or to resign on his own, with the result that the whole cabinet resigned, apparently in the hope that the Minseitō, still holding a majority, would be given a renewed mandate on the precedent of the Second Katō Cabinet in the 1920s.

Saionji, however, offered the premiership to Inukai with the suggestion that he consider a coalition cabinet, but he refused, remarking that coalition cabinets had never been a success ever since Ōkuma's in 1898 of which he retained unpleasant memories. As a result Adachi and ten members of his faction, including Nakano, Tomita, Yamaji and Kazami, seceded from the party—as Miki also did some time later. The most noteworthy refusal to secede was Nagai who, though denounced by Nakano as an opportunist, showed his usual prudence by remaining in the party, later to become a major faction leader and to reach ministerial rank in the Saitō and later cabinets.

There are signs that the seceders were expected to be much more numerous, as Inukai is said to have hoped that if Adachi could bring across 80 breakaways, he would have a majority without dissolving the House. As it was, he even refused Adachi a cabinet seat, though Kuhara urged this and went as far as resigning his post of secretary-general in protest.

Nakano's own account also indicates that he had had hopes of a happier outcome, since he speaks of the circumstances of his leaving the Minseitō as 'fortuitous' and admits having no immediate plans, though adding that his group could not have coexisted indefinitely in the party with 'bureaucratic outsiders' whose 'mandated territory' it had become. He attacks Inoue particularly in the bitterest terms saying, for example, that he is 'unequalled in combining an appearance of originality with an actual degeneracy into the politics of petty officialdom'. Resentment of Inoue's policies during the financial crisis soon led to his assassination by the agrarian Blood Brotherhood group, though any influence on them by Nakano or Kazami would seem to have been indirect, in the absence of any accusation to the contrary.

Nakano emphasises the sincerity of Kuhara and Adachi, describing Adachi as possessing an ardour and dedication capable of evoking a response from younger men and as being free from the 'Meiji bureaucratic tradition' which is Japan's greatest drawback. He adds: 'Such a hothead as myself has been tethered in the stable of the established parties for five years only for the sake of Adachi.'[64]

These last remarks suggest the broader significance of the situation in which Nakano was now placed. He and the younger faction of the Minseitō had entered politics as champions of post-war 'reconstruction' but, despite some modest achievements, had remained subordinate to their elders in party and bureaucracy. The shortcomings of the latter under the dual crisis of Chinese national resurgence and world depression might have given a younger generation with the requisite qualities a chance to pose a challenge to their control—indeed only in this way might the party system have acquired a more dynamic and creative character than the 'run-of-the-mill politics' (as it was described by Takahashi Korekiyo) which could only function in the absence of a really searching crisis. In the event, however, their resources—organisational, financial, ideological and perhaps moral—proved inadequate.

Despite his failure in party manoeuvres, Nakano as always remained convinced that a momentous national advance even greater than the Meiji Restoration was at hand—of which the Manchurian Incident would be only the prelude and during which the resources of Manchuria would provide the needed stimulus to Japan's 'renovation' under state economic control. Although he had as yet only sketchy ideas as to how the renovation would be accomplished, he was at least sure that it could not be done under a two-party system imitated from the British model.

3
Liberalism sacrificed to national solidarity

The few years following Nakano's breach with the Minseitō represent a transitional phase between his previous acceptance of party liberalism, along with the international status quo, and his later all-out advocacy of a mass-based 'totalitarianism' combined with military expansionism. His development represents a series of alert responses to the problems and opportunities presented by the period, during which the acute atmosphere of crisis engendered by the depression and the Manchurian Incident gave way to a phase of relative stability. Nakano meanwhile took a rather complex stand which on the one hand emphasised the continuing elements of crisis as an argument for national reorganisation, while on the other hand he denied that Japan faced any immediate external threat—this with a view to encouraging a confident diplomatic line. Thus, when the Saitō cabinet's foreign minister Uchida made his well-known 'scorched-earth' speech defying the League of Nations, Nakano remarked in the Diet that such rhetoric was out of proportion to the Powers' actual impotence to intervene.[65]

His overall tendency was, however, to move steadily away from his earlier adaptation to the existing political structure and towards intensifying pressure for its reorganisation, in the process reviving older arguments and attitudes which had latterly been restrained. The indiscriminate pugnacity of his *Tōhō Jiron* days was, for example, revived in an outburst at a meeting held in August 1932 to welcome Komai Tokuzō, a representative of the Manchukuo government. Here Nakano defiantly described the parties as publicly scorned for their selfish scheming, the bureaucrats as nationally resented for concentrating on their own narrow interests and the military as incurring popular disdain for their decline into military cliques, while financiers were abused as 'Zaibatsu' for lacking a sense of social responsibility. 'An uncouth man', he concluded, 'is not bound by decorum.'[66]—so proclaiming his return to the image of a rugged representative of the robust masses challenging a decadent establishment.

While maintaining his customary opposition to bureaucratic privilege and his advocacy of popular advancement, Nakano now sought to guide national political action into channels quite distinct from the established parties. Though at first experimenting with a new kind of Diet party under Adachi's leadership, he soon found it impossible to fit into joint political action in this grouping either, as if the kind of wayward impatience he had displayed in the *Asahi* was now reasserting itself. Concurrently he moved away from Diet-centred politics to concentrate on mass movements in which a growing role was played by Restorationist slogans reminiscent of those current among right wing groups like the earlier Genyōsha or, more recently, Kita Ikki's movement. At the same time, however, Nakano retained his more recently acquired emphasis on rationally devised policies and consistently rejected terrorism or putschism. He is said as a result to have been regarded by most of the 'activist right' as a 'mere debater' or a 'showman'. In one representative speech, he stressed the advantages of a responsible national movement, founded on a combination of all the productive segments of society, over the fitful and irresponsible violence of extremists (*'shishi-jinjin gōketsu no shi'*) whom he likened to unloaded packhorses rushing ahead but carrying nothing:

> If you don't restrain them with bits and fasten saddles on them, load them with goods, guns and provisions and mount riders on them, progressing in ordered columns, it does not amount to a major advance.[67]

A newer element in his political strategy was a large measure of collaboration with various factions of the army, partly with a view to enlisting their aid in social reconstruction and partly for the promotion of tougher foreign policies in relation to China and the Anglo–American bloc. He chiefly differed from them in the continued hope for an understanding with the Soviet Union and to some extent in questioning narrow military demands in the light of wider issues implied by his conception of a broad-based national movement. For example, he could express concern in the Diet that the rural relief budget was being sacrificed to demands for rearmament.

As time passed, he felt that his most pressing need was to combat tendencies to complacency arising partly from the diplomatic lull, due to the powers' failure to intervene in Manchuria (as he had predicted), and partly from economic recovery. The reimposition of the gold embargo under Inukai had produced some inflationary stimulus to the economy and under the Saitō cabinet, which retained Takahashi Korekiyo as finance minister, this was reinforced by an intensive program of deficit financing for economic relief and the expansion of armament industries, through which the worst effects of the depression were alleviated fairly rapidly. During 1933 the resulting export boom raised Japan to the world's first place as a textile exporter.

Under these conditions Nakano stressed the hollowness of the economy which he described as still haunted by the 'spectre of economic and industrial anarchy under the name of liberalism'[68] and during this period gave first priority to internal reconstruction as against international issues. Although he expected that the latter would ultimately again become acute, he meanwhile regarded national reorganisation as the precondition for their final solution. This line of thought in general agreed with that of Ishiwara Kanji, a key figure in the Manchurian Incident, who became one of the closest of his army contacts and hoped for a fairly long period of peace in order to develop Japan's strategic potential before the ultimate international showdown.

Thus, although Nakano still persisted in the Pan-Asian theme, he treated it in terms of long term objectives rather than immediate issues. This is illustrated by a speaking tour on the 'Greater Asia Monroe Doctrine', which he conducted in June 1933 and included a meeting addressed jointly with Ras Bihari Bose. Here he surveyed the historical background of the idea, embracing Sun Yat-sen's 'Greater Asianism', the success of the United States' Monroe Doctrine in the Western Hemisphere, the Ōkuma government's mistake in courting Britain and oppressing China and the Versailles 'fiasco' resulting from Japan's failure to utilise the war to promote Asian revolt.

He contrasted the case of General Tanaka, who in 1922 had hoped that the United States would hold the Philippines so as not to arouse hopes of independence among Japan's colonies, with the enlightened attitude of Ishiwara, who favoured the reversion of the South Manchurian Railway concessions to Manchukuo. The white race had preempted the earth's surface by wielding the weapons of science and was trying to perpetuate the situation by its system of treaties. It was therefore Japan's mission to lead the oppressed peoples in revolt and the founding of Manchukuo was already bearing fruit in that it had checkmated Soviet pressure on the Far East and diverted it towards India, to the discomfiture of Britain.[69]

Despite Nakano's concern with mass agitation, he continued to widen his financial contacts, apparently by convincing some business circles that he could help them in a situation where their traditional base in the parties was decaying, while they were simultaneously under fire from ultranationalists for such unJapanese practices as 'dollar-buying' and from army-centred elements aiming at strict economic reorganisation in the interests of the 'national defence state'. Under these conditions, Nakano's proposals for economic controls with the cooperation of private industrial and financial organisations was a more moderate alternative, which also largely agreed with the Zaibatsu's own current program of reorganisation and rationalisation, replacing family proprietorship with corporate management, in which Ikeda Seihin was taking the lead. In regard to the terrorist threat too, which had claimed the life of Mitsui's Baron Dan, Nakano could be of service, as it was he who arranged for Ikeda to pay Kita Ikki and others the regular protection money which apparently kept most of the right inactive on this front. In testifying later about this, as well as about political contributions to Nakano, Ikeda described him as: 'A rising statesman with particularly advanced ideas.'[70]

In addition to Ikeda's circle and the shipping magnate Yamashita Kamesaburō, Nakano was regularly backed by Tsuda Shingo, president of the major textile concern Kanebō in Osaka. On the death of his original financial backer Yasukawa Keiichirō in 1934, he continued to receive the support of his son Daigorō whose main interests were in electric power. Nakano had helped him as vice-minister of communications and the two later regularly cooperated in relation to proposals for the national control of electric power—an issue much debated during the mid-thirties. Another backer interested in this field was Matsunaga Yasuzaemon, a onetime electoral rival.

It was probably financial support from such quarters that enabled Nakano to build the new house in Yoyogi which he entered early in 1932 and remained his home thereafter. Its cost is usually said to have been met by royalties from some of his father-in-law Miyake's publications, though one source represents Kita as rebuking Nakano for such a tame explanation of his new appearance of prosperity. The house was apparently well-appointed and his 'bodyguard' Terada is said to have advised him on security aspects.

Certainly, at least during the 1930s, Nakano shows every sign of being financially better off than at any earlier time. Another example is his developing equestrian interests. He took up horse-riding seriously after a visit to Manchukuo in 1932, during which he had to do much of his travelling on horseback and found it unexpectedly congenial. For this purpose, General Araki, then war minister, had an improved artificial leg designed for him by the army medical service. He is mentioned as having during the 1930s acquired at least nine horses, including two thoroughbreds (one from Kazami's financial backer and one through army contacts), so making him the equal in number and quality of horses of any private equestrian in Japan at the time.

Later in 1936 he established a well-appointed riding club humourously called the Tōfūkai (East Wind Club—an allusion to the proverb 'the east wind to a horse's ears', an equivalent to 'water off a duck's back'). Here he stabled the horses of fellow enthusiasts as well as his own. His son Yasuo comments that this satisfied his father's intensely competitive spirit, though he and his brother Tatsuhiko wondered suspiciously how he could afford such horses and facilities. Horsemanship also formed his main continuing bond with Ogata who relates that, in view of their growing divergence on political issues, they once agreed not to speak on any other subject, in order not to injure their personal friendship.

Nakano's growing extremism is often partly attributed to a series of personal tragedies which occurred about this time and may well have contributed to the peculiar intensity that marked many of his later activities. The first was the loss of his eldest son Katsuaki in 1931 in a skiing accident, on which Nakano wrote a pensive account of the circumstances and his own reactions.[71] He mentions that Kita was one of the mourners and comforted him in his remorse at having, on first hearing of the accident, sent his son a curt telegram saying only: 'Be brave ... Father.' Kita described the blunt directness of the message as 'a passionate expression of manly affection' for which the son must have been deeply grateful during his last painful hours. Ogata headed the customary committee in charge of funeral arrangements and continued to do the same for every funeral occurring in the family, including Nakano's own.

In June 1934 Nakano's wife died of tuberculosis after the better part of a year's fluctuating illness. As already noted, she had used what influence she possessed to encourage him to follow a more conventional political career and she never agreed with the change in his attitudes beginning from the Manchurian Incident. She had also habitually defended such old associates of his as Inukai and Wakatsuki when he was infuriated with them. He did not write anything about her death, as he had about his son's, but personally chose her death-name and, though never given to religious observances or interests of any kind, often recited the short Heart Sutra (*Hannya Shingyō*) for her at the family shrine.

There is no indication that he ever took any further interest in women so that politics, which had always been his dominant interest, now became his sole emotional outlet. Another mark of austere dedication was his abstinence from alcohol in his later years.

Next, about a year later, his second son Yūshi died. He had grown rebellious after his mother's death, and following the example of his uncle Hideto preferred an artistic career and despised all politics. He once induced his father to accompany him to see a foreign film '*Nero the Tyrant*' and tried to make the point that Japan was now as corrupt as Nero's Rome. He was finally given psychiatric treatment for signs of mental disturbance and, while taking a rest cure at the family beach house at Negishi, suffered a cut which led to his death from blood poisoning. Nakano had by then, however, placed all his hopes on his youngest son Yasuo, as the third son Tatsuhiko was also quite sceptical about politics. Until Yasuo was older, the only interest Nakano shared with his sons was horse-riding.

The Kokumin Dōmei

In his pamphlet of early 1932, 'Trends of Japan in Transition' (*Tenkan Nihon no Dōkō*), Nakano admits that, owing to the suddenness of their breach with the Minseitō, he and his associates so far had no definite plans, but he goes on to sketch some basic principles which he favoured. These, he claims, are not essentially different from the principles they had supported in the Minseitō, but recent events had further underlined the need for drastic change in modes of politicial action.

In an age of intensifying nationalism, he says, there is a general shift towards one-party systems designed to harmonise national interests and promote them on a world scale. This means that the existing two-party system on the British model, catering for competing interests and principles, is now outmoded. The rival 'positive' and 'negative' financial policies of the Seiyūkai and Minseitō now belong equally to the dying world of 'Adam Smith economics', while their respective 'strong' and 'weak' foreign policies are equally bankrupt. The projected coalition cabinet had been designed to meet the situation by state control of the economy and a foreign policy of 'autonomous conciliation'. He is now thinking in terms of a philosophy of 'social nationalism' of which he writes:

> Nationalism is to be emphasised with a view to acting on international society ... Social nationalism, with a view to the rational control of international society, demands the establishment on the globe of the principles of racial equality and free access to natural resources.[72]

He takes care to distinguish it from state socalism, which was being put forward in various forms. One was associated with Kita's 'reorganisation plan', while another appeared in he rightward-tending section of the proletarian movement as represented by Akamatsu Katsumaro, which had seen the Manchurian Incident, together with the pressures favouring social reform among elements of the armed forces, as offering a means to challenge the existing capitalist order to an extent that the Marxist-oriented labour movement had not been able to achieve. Nakano comments:

> Japan's future will not be realised nor the welfare of mankind advanced by the mere control by state socialism of our tiny island kingdom on the lines of a miniature garden ... It is not a matter of socialism based on the State but of a nationalism having society as its object.[73]

Although a party based on this program would still engage in parliamentary politics, it would not be narrowly committed to majority rule but rather conceived in terms of an elite capable of giving a dynamic lead. Nakano was indebted for the term 'social nationalism' to his long-standing friend Professor Sugimori of Waseda, who was becoming his chief adviser on ideological matters. He did not, however, make much use of this term in subsequent discussion, or do much to explore it theoretical implications, as he gave most of his attention to concrete issues and policies as occasion demanded.

In the election of February 1932, which resulted in a landslide victory for the Seiyūkai, he and Kazami were comfortably returned, though only five candidates directly endorsed by Adachi gained election.

After Inukai's assassination, to which he referred in rather muted terms of regret, Nakano's immediate hopes were to have Adachi included in the succeeding non-party cabinet under Admiral Saitō, but without success. Their group therefore devoted their efforts over the next few months to establishing a formal party organisation which was inaugurated late in the year under the name of the Kokumin Dōmei (National League). The main participants were 32 members of the House of Representatives, two of the House of Peers and thirteen former Representatives. Almost all were ex-members of the Minseitō, many no doubt discouraged by the party's election debacle. It had been hoped also to recruit elements of Akamatsu's 'social fascist' group but there turned out to be too little common ground, as Akamatsu aimed at a much more complete program of socialisation and was markedly hostile to the Zaibatsu.

Adachi naturally became the party president, with Nakano as chief director and Yamaji as secretary-general. The main function in the inaugural ceremony was the presentation by Adachi of the party's manifesto and platform. The latter read:

1 The spirit on which the nation was founded will be developed, aiming at the restoration of international justice.

2   A controlled economy will be established, aiming at the guarantee of the masses' livelihood.
3   The accumulated evils of the political world will be eliminated, aiming at the full realisation of a national political program.[74]

Under the first heading Adachi condemned economic inequality and racist immigration laws, which were to be remedied by an accord between the existing economic blocs, since these had to be accepted as a fact of life. The second plank he described as distinct both from decadent capitalism, with its anti-social tendencies, and from socialism which, with its insistence on nationalisation, forfeits the efficiency only to be attained through the creativity of individuals and organisations. The third goal was to be achieved by replacing the cabinet system with a Council of State (*Kokumuin*).

> Departments have fallen into a state of separatism, rivalry, lack of control and mutual contradiction, knowing no source of coordination and unity. The Council of State advocated by the Kokumin Dōmei will be a powerful organ composed of a small number of Ministers of State entrusted with the duty of constitutional assistance to the Sovereign and capable of establishing and enforcing broad national policies. Government departments are to be headed by directors, instead of ministers, and these will perform administrative duties under the direction of the Council of State, clearly distinguishing between the political and administrative spheres.[75]

The criticism of the current process of government, which has elsewhere been described as 'a shift to a highly bureaucratic system characterised by a remarkable decentralisation of power among the respective ministers of state',[76] seems accurate enough. The remedies proposed reflect the development of Nakano's thought along lines suggested by Cole, but with a stronger insistence on the role of the state in mobilising national power in the context of world crisis.

As a means of heightening the impact of its establishment, the Kokumin Dōmei adopted the rather novel feature (for Japan) of having its members wear a semi-military type of uniform of black serge with a belt—though Adachi himself did not join in this practice. Branch activities were initiated in Osaka, Hyōgo, Fukuoka, Kumamoto and Kōchi—areas where the leadership had their main contacts. A climax was reached in February 1933, when Nakano held a 'national rally' at Hibiya to advocate leaving the League of Nations, in anticipation of its acceptance of the Lytton report on Manchuria. This was followed up by his speaking tour on the 'Greater Asia Monroe Doctrine', mentioned earlier.

Although the Kokumin Dōmei was later looked back on as having made the first moves leading to the collapse of party liberalism, and in its early days there was widespread expectation that Nakano's activities would lead to a 'supra-party national movement', the party soon lost its initial drive. This was doubtless partly due to the easing of the atmosphere of crisis but also happened because many of its members, notably Yamaji, as professional politicians found mass agitation uncongenial and preferred to think in terms of manoeuvres between the two major parties in the Diet. Nakano therefore, though for the time remaining in the party, began to build up an independent system of connections which he hoped would more readily suit his political style, as will be described later.

The Okada cabinet, formed the following year, was boycotted by the Seiyūkai but supported by the Minseitō, and most of the Kokumin Dōmei under Yamaji's lead were disposed to take the latter course. They also unsuccessfully tried to have Adachi appointed colonial minister but all such moves were opposed by Nakano in favour of oppositionism. His final breach with the party came when Adachi so far compromised with the 'status quo party' as to join the Cabinet Council (*Naikaku Shingikai*) which Okada set up in May 1935. This included representatives of the Minseitō, the House of Peers, the armed services and industry, being intended to provide more policy continuity between cabinets, though its scope was limited by the exclusion of defence and foreign policy matters.

In an article 'Looking to Adachi', Nakano ironically wished him success, remarking that Adachi was too old to join in what he would look on as his own 'children's politics'. Nakano, for his part, would have preferred Adachi to become another of the heroes whom the latter had recently been so occupied in enshrining in his Hall of the Eight Sages at Yokohama and in that of the Three Heroes at Kumamoto. The Eight Sages were the Buddha, Confucius, Christ, Socrates, Prince Shōtoku, Kōbō Daishi, Shinran and Nichiren, the first four representing respectively Eastern and Western religion and philosophy, and the last four Japan. The local 'Three Heroes' were Kikuchi Taketoki, Katō Kiyomasa and Hosokawa Shigekata. Defining his own position in relation to Adachi, Nakano states:

> If by politics is meant taking one's stand on the status quo and merely patching it up, I find that at some stage or other I have slipped out of the category of what is called politics and come to participate instead in the renovating enterprise of national reconstruction.[77]

His accompanying criticisms of the Council as an inadequate substitute for a national mass movement, and of Adachi for joining it, were strikingly similar to his earlier reactions when Inukai had joined Terauchi's Foreign Policy Deliberation Committee. Nakano compared the Council to 'a stagnant pool formed when the post-Manchuria flood tide was trapped by a rock barrier'. Among its members, his associate Ikeda of Mitsui was himself able but the setting was too negative to achieve much.

Nakano and his immediate following formally left the Kokumin Dōmei late in 1935. Kazami, who had backed him in the struggle with Yamaji, did the same but from then on followed an independent course and was later to rise to prominence in Prince Konoe's 'brain trust'.

National action and the Tōhōkai

As Nakano became convinced during 1933 that the Kokumin Dōmei would not fulfil the role he had projected for it, he increasingly devoted himself to independent action, though for the time retaining his party affiliation in the Diet and for other purposes where it was useful. This new phase was indicated in a speech entitled 'Manifesto of Strong Politics', in which he spoke forcefully of the need for a dynamic political drive to cut through the existing tangle of capitalistic and communistic ideologies and interest groups. Under such conditions, a liberalistic appeal to public opinion was no better than sailing a compassless ship. 'Politicians exist for the sake of the masses', he declared, in striking contrast to the credo of both the official orthodoxy and the right, which regarded all loyalty and service as being directed primarily to the Emperor. But, he continued, the masses' needs are not revealed by the results of corrupt elections. The weakness of the Seiyūkai with its huge Diet majority was due to the lack of a powerful national movement behind it. He suggested that such a movement might be based on functional groups coordinated on lines comparable to Lenin's 'democratic centralism'. The central political organ, a Council of State of seven members, should not be concerned with specialist functions but with broader principles—so eliminating the current departmental factionalism and, even more important, the problematic status of the Supreme Command, with its privilege of 'direct access to the Emperor'.

> His Majesty's armed forces are at the same time the nation's armed forces and are founded on the nation's masses. Statesmen should joined hands with the military only via the nation's masses.[78]

This last, it may be noted, contrasts with Kita's scheme for reform via direct military initiative, which was widely shared by many in the state socialist camp, including Akamatsu.

Nakano's vehicle for his efforts in this direction was the Tōhōkai (Orient Society) which, as noted, had earlier been revived among *Gakan* staff largely on Kazami's initiative. This body was now given more definite form by renting a house in Akasaka as its headquarters, though Nakano long insisted that it was still not a political association but a society for the study of cultural questions and current affairs. By this means he avoided any direct clash with the Kokumin Dōmei but, even after breaking with that body, long retained this definition of the Tōhōkai to distinguish it from all parties in the accepted sense— rather on the lines adopted for the old Kakushin Club. He did, however, state that, when the time came for more clearly political action, he hoped to set up a separate Orient Reconstruction League (*Tōhō Kaizō Dōmei*) for this purpose.

In the Tōhōkai he brought together both activists and special advisers. Among these, Professor Sugimori, as noted, was his adviser on political theory; on diplomacy he was advised by Honda Kumatarō, a senior China expert who had taken part in the former Tōhōkai, and Nakayama Masaru, a younger man for whom he had found a post under Shidehara. His expert on economics was Kojima Seiichi, who had established his own Institute of Economics, while his principal military adviser was Ishiwara Kanji, whom he had contacted after his 1932 visit to Manchukuo and was closely associated with for some years. Ishiwara was a wide-ranging student of military history and strategic theory, but was also to some extent impelled by the vision of an apocalyptic world crisis which drew some of its force from an interest in Nichiren Buddhism, shared with Kita—though this was one feature that did not appeal to Nakano. The coolness he habitually showed towards mysticism or religious emotion of any kind was, after all, consistent with his basically Neo-Confucian background. Ishiwara, for his part, for some time found Nakano a useful spokesman, since he himself as a professional soldier could not take much part in open political activity, apart from some pamphlets.

As another component in his political network the journal *Gakan* was converted into Nakano's propaganda organ the following year. His case for its reorganisation was facilitated by its continuous losses since the Manchurian Incident and by October 1934 he had obtained Miyake's agreement to the arrangement. His secretary Shintō Kazuma was appointed editor and publisher, with regular help from the economist Kojima—whose name often appears in the journal in various capacities. The October issue was therefore advertised as a 'Rebirth and Advance Number' and from then on Nakano wrote monthly political commentaries for it, as well as other material. The texts closely follow those of his speeches in the Diet and elsewhere.

With help from his experts, Nakano in late 1933 compiled the most comprehensive statement ever of his political and economic program, entitled 'Outline Plan for National Reconstruction' (*Kokka Kaizō Keikaku Kōryō*). It seems largely conceived as a counter proposal to Kita's *Outline Plan for the Reconstruction of Japan*. Apart from the similarity in title, it is drawn up in a schematic manner resembling Kita's, each chapter consisting of a series of propositions in formal literary diction accompanied by commentaries in more vernacular style. In view of the following that Kita's thought had attracted among young officers critical of the existing system, it was natural for Nakano to make his own bid for a share of such support. Besides, despite Nakano's personal association with Kita, described by Shintō as a 'regular exchange of ideas',[79] there were various aspects of Kita's proposals which did not appeal to him, such as the nationalisation of large-scale enterprises and the conception of 'activating the Emperor's prerogatives' through martial law as the key political lever for enacting reform.

The body of Nakano's *Outline Plan* begins with an introduction pointing out that, as it is intended to deal with an emergency situation, the plan is not a 'design for Utopia'. Taking as a model the metabolism of the human body (a recurring metaphor), it envisages simultaneous processes of partial destruction and construction in a sequence determined by empirical needs, contrary to the manner of 'formulistic desk theorists'. Nevertheless, it adds, the plan is unified by the general principle of state economic control.

This is a clear contrast, on the one hand, to Kita's plan for preplanned reconstruction after a single decisive coup and, on the other, to his great range of social proposals such as the use of Esperanto in education and those relating to the status of women. Regarding educational reform, Nakano mentions in a preface that he appreciates its importance but will leave a treatment of it to a later date. Under the existing conditions of thought control this was, of course, a dangerous topic and he finally never gave it any special attention.

Nakano's specific proposals consist of nine chapters, of which the first is entitled 'Declaration of a State of Emergency'. In this he criticises the recent Takahashi financial policy of 'uncontrolled inflation' for relief works and armaments. The latter aspect brings the spectre of war closer, especially when combined with international tensions over trade, since while currency depreciation makes Japan's exports more competitive, it also invites economic retaliation. In these conditions, the assumptions underlying liberalism and the party system collapse. Public alarm at the situation is being shown in widespread sympathy for Inukai's assassins and the solution lies in a synthesis between their 'tragic passion' and more constructive principles.

In chapter 2 of this work 'Reform of the Political Structure', in contrast to Kita's reliance on martial law and the Reservists' Association, Nakano proposes the delegation, through due legal process by the Diet, of dictatorial powers to a cabinet for a fixed term of years. He claims that he does not deny democracy (*minshushugi*) in principle but, since the parties, as the 'puppets of corrupt capitalism', are beyond redemption, they must be left out of account. The slogan should be: 'Democracy as end and dictatorship as means.' The Diet would not be suspended (as in Kita's plan) but restricted to the 'surveillance of government functions' until the Diet itself is reconstructed. This would be achieved partly by a new electoral system emphasising occupational representation (giving a 'three-dimensional scale model of the living nation'), with geographical representation from large multi-member constituencies accounting for no more than 20 per cent of Diet membership.

It may be noted that the Kokumin Dōmei's more radical proposal for the abolition of cabinet has been dropped, probably owing to the example of Germany earlier in the year, when Hitler had been delegated dictatorial powers for five years. In this chapter, however, Nakano points out that, apart from 'extreme precedents' such as Germany and Italy, similar measures are being taken in the 'democratic United States'—in the New Deal. He was still far from his later unreserved admiration for the Axis powers.

The remaining chapters all deal with aspects of the economic controls to be exercised by the dictatorship. Chapter 3 outlines the general principles of this program and follows the lines, largely inspired by Nakano's study of Cole, introduced earlier in *The Rebirth of Stagnating Japan*. Defining his position as 'a revision of capitalism', he explains his conception of a controlled economy as being not state management or socialisation (which means bureaucratisation and rigidity), but private management under state guidance, which would foster private enterprise by offering inducements from the standpoint of promoting the general welfare. It would be coordinated by an Economic General Staff (Cole's expression), consisting of an Economic Policy Council, together with auxiliary organs for investigation, planning and supervision, as well as an advisory body representing interest groups, for example, industrial organisations and labour.

The remaining chapters amplify these principles for banking (featuring Cole's Board of National Investment), commerce and industry (geared to the Asian Bloc conception rather than the traditional 'export first' policy and utilising associations of each class of enterprise), agriculture, public finance (with joint public–private utilities along the lines of Nakano's telecommunications plan), labour and integration with Manchukuo.

This *Outline Plan*, though compact, clearly placed Nakano in the spectrum of contemporary political thought, on the one hand rejecting surviving tendencies toward political and economic liberalism and, on the other, distinguishing his standpoint from other varieties of reformism including Marxism, state socialism and complete subservience to strategic military planning. His general rationality also contrasts with the more sentimental forms of Restorationism or Japanism, whether expressed in the 'Imperial Way' ideology of a purely spiritual revival within existing institutions, or in the Agrarianist argument for local autonomy and a return to primitivism. He also avoids any suggestion of change through coup or terrorism, towards which strong tendencies existed.

Nakano never departed from the theoretical basis outlined here, though in pursuit of its application he grew to rely ever more heavily on emotion-charged agitation and an appeal to war hysteria, which fially tended to converge with traditional Restorationism, *bushidō* and associated themes.

The aspect left most open in his plan was the question of how the dictatorship was to be established. It would be difficult to realise on a legal basis without some support from the bureaucracy and any influence of Nakano's in such circles through the Minseitō was no longer in evidence. In particular, there is little sign of contact with the rising school of 'new bureaucrats' who were those most concerned with revisionist thought within the Establishment. He regularly disparaged them, as in one Diet speech where he challenged the new bureaucrats to take more seriously the philosophy of the study society then serving as their focus—the Kokuikai (National Order Society), which claimed to be based on Yōmeigaku.[80] His only alternative was to build up a following in other sectors of society against the day when the Establishment's failings would be exposed by crisis and a radical shift in the power structure would become feasible.

About the time of compiling the *Outline Plan*, Nakano found an encouraging opening to wider influence by being elected Policy Director (*Tōrei*) of a union of communications ministry employees, the Teiyū Dōshikai. This link with organised labour was a good counterpart to Kazami's action in the rural sector. The union had previously been headed by Akamatsu and affiliated to the social democratic Sōdōmei, reaching a membership of 3500 by 1932. In April of that year, having turned to state socialism, Akamatsu disaffiliated from the Sōdōmei but a majority of members later revolted against his political preoccupations and 'reactionary Japanism' and his faction seceded. The new Executive Committee, chaired by a man who conveniently came from Nakano's home town, then created the office of

Policy Director, to be filled by a prominent public figure whose influence might be helpful. Nakano was chosen, despite some ideological misgivings, because of his background as a vice-minister, and perhaps also owing to Adachi's efforts to pass trade union legislation under the Minseitō government.

In an address accepting the appointment, Nakano surveyed the history of the Japanese labour movement, saying that, although the workers and farmers were the very marrow of the Japanese race ('Japanese among Japanese'), their organisational expression had been distrusted and suppressed largely because they had not developed principles adequate to gain national recognition. These should have been based on experience, Japanese tradition and the international environment but, instead, the labour movement since the First World War had been dominated by foreign-influenced intelligentsia, who had first undermined it with impractical theorising and irresponsible tactics and then, under persecution, abandoned it in 'recantation' (*tenkō*). The solution for labour, in the light of existing conditions, was to devote its efforts primarily to the advancement of the collective national power, combating capitalism insofar as it obstructed this and rejecting communism entirely. Only within this framework could labour's interests be properly served.

This would be achieved through a system of industrial associations combining capital and labour, in which collective bargaining would be allowed but both strikes and sackings ruled out by compulsory state arbitration. The military would be a powerful ally in achieving reform because they were coming to realise that national strength is derived from social justice. Although, Nakano said, in world history generally the military have been protectors of conservatism, in Japan they were now allying themselves with progressive forces for national reconstruction.[81]

Nakano also became president of a Yawata steelworks union called the Yawata Kinrō Dōmei, with a membership of 3700, but in less than a year his standing with the labour movement was undermined by unfavourable developments in the Teiyū Dōshikai. After his appointment, the union leadership launched a militant campaign, relying on Nakano's influence to protect them from retaliation. This, however, now proved insufficient, as the chairman and three others were dismissed for obstruction of operations, breach of discipline and neglect of duties. Although Nakano's efforts for their reinstatement were unavailing, he refused to authorise a strike, which did not agree with his principles, and promised instead a political struggle against the 'real culprits', the Saitō cabinet, which, he said, could not survive long. This proved to be true for other reasons but Nakano's credibility was weakened and he was obliged to resign when the majority of members voted to reaffiliate with the Sōdōmei against his opposition. The union, however, soon lost the bulk of its members to a rival grouping.

This was a major setback to Nakano's plans for a broad national movement, especially at a time when the climate was now less favourable to change, since the easing in the overall crisis was being widely noted. One sign of this was Finance Minister Takahashi's decision to restrain the rate of inflation, which meant cutting down on rural relief and armament expansion. Both aspects were criticised by General Araki but Takahashi was backed by the new Foreign Minister Hirota Kōki, who favoured a new phase of conciliatory diplomacy. Although Hirota had been associated with the Genyōsha in his youth, he had (contrary to widespread assumptions which led to his execution as a war criminal) lost all connection with it during his career as a professional diplomat. As a result of their stand, as well as criticism of his factionalism in army appointments, Araki resigned as War Minister early in 1934.

Particularly as the parties also hoped that an admitted passing of the crisis would entail the restoration of party cabinets, Nakano now systematically attacked all the government's claims to economic recovery and diplomatic stabilisation. He began with a Diet interpellation which he also published as a pamphlet entitled: 'The Empire's Emergency is far from Resolved' (*Teikoku no Hijōji danjite kaishō sezu*). In it, he rebukes Hirota for his flippancy in the Diet when, on Nakano's raising the question of an Asian Monroe doctrine, he replied that Japan could not have one, as there was no Monroe in Japan. In refutation of Hirota's stand, he reviews the situation in China where, as a result of boycotts, the United States had supplanted Japan as chief trading partner and was now developing air routes which would pose a future military threat.

Regarding the economy, he denies that the export boom had helped the overall situation. It merely amounted to the undervalued selling of Japan's labour and resources, like postwar Germany's 'hunger export', while the workers and farmers suffered from inflated domestic prices. Abroad, it had led to retaliation like the abrogation of the Japan–India Commercial Treaty. Again, industrialisation by armament expansion has its limitations, since military demand does not involve regular consumption and when requirements were satisfied the new industries would have to find export outlets.

Although Nakano had expected Agriculture Minister Gotō Fumio, like Araki, to resign at the cuts in relief spending, he was disgusted to hear him 'cheerfully' broadcasting on New Year's Day about the superiority of Japan's National Polity and the gratitude owed the Imperial House. 'What thick-skinned characters these bureaucrats are!—I thought.' Actually, Nakano adds, the National Polity of the Single Sovereign and Myriad People should be realised in the economic sphere through an organic, corporate community. This was much along Kita's line.

After the Saitō cabinet fell later in the year through the manoeuvres of Baron Hiranuma's Establishment rightwing machine in the justice ministry, Nakano maintained the same posture towards the succeeding Okada cabinet, which marked a further advance in the emergence of the 'new bureaucrats'. Okada, he wrote, had merely been given the task of controlling the military, playing down the emergency and soothing Japan in a 'fool's paradise'.

> Among the powers [having mentioned Germany, Italy and the USA] in extraordinary times (*hijōji*) we see extraordinary figures (*hijōjimbutsu*) displaying their vigour but in our country's crisis we have seen the emergence of a dwarf cabinet not to be entertained even in ordinary times.[82]

In the next Diet he continued his attacks on economic policies. Attacking Takahashi (again Finance Minister) in quite personal terms ('there is nothing so frightening as an old man's conceit') he compared the alternation of deflationary and inflationary policies with the similar fluctuations under the late Tokugawa regime. Just as that had ended in collapse and been followed by the Restoration, he said, 'the present industrial feudalism centred on the rich will be overthrown and the Industrial Restoration will be sure to follow'.[83] This was even more in Kita's vein.

Nakano was encouraged the following year by the government's embarrassment at the mass hysteria produced by the 'Emperor as Organ' controversy, which was launched by Hiranuma's machine against Dr Minobe's theory that the Emperor was the supreme organ of the state rather than the locus of sovereignty, so providing a rationale for liberalist politics. Although Nakano did not take a clear stand on the issue itself, he hoped that the protest movement held possibilities for national reconstruction. In a historical survey, he treats the earlier theories of Hozumi and Uesugi opposing the Organ Theory as having favoured the clan oligarchs, while Minobe's theory had been utilised by the then rising liberals who now, as represented by Prince Saionji, Lord Privy Seal Makino and Privy Council President Ichiki, occupy the seats of power in their turn. With the decline of party power, the cooling of reformist zeal in the upper levels of the army (which Nakano was beginning to recognise) and the cautious attitude of the Zaibatsu, these elders now dominate the political process, using the Emperor as a shield through the Organ Theory and producing cabinets of 'weak reactionary type' (elsewhere described as 'reactionary liberalism').[84]

Although, he continues, the attacking rightwing activists may be open to criticism as recalling the old oligarchic Hozumi theory, they are not primarily concerned with legal theories but rather with eliminating the 'liberalistic status quo party'. Tōyama Mitsuru, their 'high priest', has said: 'The Constitution in my heart is far greater and more boundless than the Constitution written by someone like Itō.' So he rejects all such formulae, including Hozumi's as well.

> His aim is to seek out the ultimate principle on which the nation was founded, doing away with fashionable legalistic theorists. The movement to destroy the 'Emperor as Organ' theory does not amount to a theory for interpreting the Constitution but an overflow from the spirit of reconstruction thundering through our age.[85]

Such hopes that the movement to 'clarify the National Polity' might serve the cause of social reconstruction, which were drawing Nakano back to a closer relationship with Tōyama, turned out in time to be seriously misplaced. This movement, whose chief theorist was Minoda Kyōki of the journal *Genri Nippon*, would rather serve to divert much of the energy of extremist nationalism away from any association with 'reconstruction' by substituting the merely conceptual goal of a spiritual purification of existing institutions. So overall, though with certain tensions, it would tend to buttress the official 'defence state' structure, combining military, new bureaucrats and Zaibatsu, which in turn was promoted by a new phase of mounting international tension.

Nakano's evolution was also affected by this setting. Having on the one hand met such limited success in his campaign for national reconstruction from within and, on the other, witnessing dramatic new conflicts in East and West, he came to reverse his priorities. Although earlier, like Kita, seeing internal reconstruction as a precondition for effective international action, he now came to view international crisis as the only lever strong enough to force internal change. This in turn implied further development in his relationship with the armed forces which now needs to be reviewed in more detail.

Relations with the military

As already noted, Nakano's approach to elements of the military had begun in the few years preceding the Manchurian Incident. Previously he had always opposed military intervention in politics as a flagrant expression of clan oligarchy but, through such contacts as Araki and

Nagata, he had become aware of the rise of new elements in the armed forces. When these then precipitated the Manchurian Incident, which to him seemed the breakthrough needed both in the international situation and in the internal stalemate faced by party politics, he drew very close to them. His manoeuvres for a coalition cabinet were linked with military circles and, even after this failure, he worked energetically for the recognition of Manchukuo, also evidently in close collaboration with them.

One example relates to a visit to Japan in mid-1932 by the Manchukuo secretary of communications, Ting Chien-hsiu, his former fellow student at Waseda, with whom he had made his first visit to the mainland. Besides giving a press conference urging recognition, at which his Japanese advisers conspicuously supplied all the answers, Ting visited Nakano's home and gave him the greater part of ¥100 000 with which he had been entrusted to promote the cause of Manchukuo in Japan.[86]

Soon afterwards another such visit was made by the Manchukuo government's secretary-general, Komai Tokuzō, who had originally been sent by War Vice-Minister Koiso to set up a civilian political division in the Kwantung Army and had risen spectacularly in the new regime under army patronage. At a reception held to welcome him, Nakano denounced reported moves to have him replaced from Japan which, he claimed, would lead to Manchukuo's becoming a refuge for worn-out bureaucrats who would undo the successes of the young officers and adventurers who had established the state. He also warned against a 'weak policy of conciliating the Chinese' (an allusion to the late Inukai's peace moves), which would lead to no better results than Shidehara had achieved. In the same month he called in the Diet for a declaration of resoluteness in support of Manchukuo, which was in fact soon afterwards recognised.

At the same time, Nakano hardly wished to become a mere client of the armed forces and regularly made statements qualifying his identification with them. He would, for example, as noted earlier, deny that rearmament was a sound basis for industrialisation, or seek to demonstrate that he was no mere flatterer of the armed forces by recalling his attacks on General Tanaka for 'mistaken thinking and avoidance of responsibility'. As already indicated, he hoped to achieve a symbiosis between the military and his conception of a civilian national movement—a stand encouraged by Araki's slogan of the 'unity of soldiers and farmers'. On the one hand, he could encourage the labour movement to look to the military as an agent of social reform, unique in the world, while on the other he could speak of the Supreme Command as integrated into a comprehensive national movement.

One controversial issue involving the military on which he took a complex stand was the reorganisation of administrative organs relating to Manchuria, undertaken by the Okada cabinet. Under this measure, all functions exercised by the foreign and colonial ministries were transferred to a Manchurian Affairs Office, headed by the War Minister, while the commander-in-chief of the Kwantung Army would concurrently hold the posts of ambassador to Manchukuo and governor of Kwantung, the original Japanese leased territory. Civil police duties were to be transferred from the colonial ministry to the military police—a move against which the ministry staff in Kwantung protested by resigning *in toto*.

Although this is another issue on which Nakano was later represented as anti-military, an article written by him at the time declared his neutrality between the army and the ministry, blaming only the cabinet for its clumsy handling of the problem.[87] He added, however, that Japan did not exist for the colonial ministry but the ministry for Japan. It could be dismantled without loss but its staff should be of use to the Manchukuo administration and should be recruited to its service, while the foreign ministry consular staff—now quite useless—could be transferred to more constructive duties in the 'southern regions.' He did not object to the commander-in-chief's serving as ambassador, but opposed making the army responsible for all phases of administration since 'swords are not suited to cooking' and even Saigō would not have shone in such a role. The implication that the Manchukuo administration should be allowed greater initiative agreed with Ishiwara's views, though Nakano went on to condemn the tendency for it to be taken over by career bureaucrats from Japan—a stand hardly consistent with his plan for colonial ministry staff.

His representation as anti-militarist on this issue stems from postwar accounts by Mitamura Takeo, a later close colleague who was active in the ministry's protest movement. In recalling his own campaign against the army plan,[88] Mitamura describes his first meeting with Nakano at the time and claims that he sympathised with him to the extent of contributing expenses. Whatever the exact circumstances, their contact did lead to his joining Nakano's movement and becoming his right-hand man in the Diet, as well as carrying on something of Nakano's tradition after the war. But in view of Mitamura's other account, that he only joined Nakano in early 1936,[89] the suggestion of earlier collaboration on the Manchuria issue seems doubtful.

Nakano repeated his arguments in a Diet interpellation, in which he also discussed another matter bearing on the army's possible role in social reform. This concerned the recent army pamphlet 'Basic

Theory of National Defence and Suggestions for its Strengthening'. Answering criticisms by the major parties that it represented military intervention in politics contrary to Emperor Meiji's Rescript to the Armed Services, Nakano claimed that this form of public expression was better than resorting to pistols and bombs as in Inukai's assassination. Referring to the pamphlet's contention that 'the individualistic economic system is bankrupt, the state bears responsibility for the livelihood of the whole nation and military power must be nourished on this basis', he argued that such a philosophy was now so commonly accepted in the new economic thought that to expound it was not a matter of politics but of educating the public. Calling on the war minister to accept responsibility for implementing the pamphlet's proposals, he said:

> This is a different matter from speeches made by futile, powerless politicians in their playhouse! This is the army which carried through the Manchurian Incident! This is the army which by its strength overturned the traditional diplomacy of submission! So the masses expect you to go ahead. Once you have spoken, merely to speak is not enough![90]

But only a few months later he was to express disappointment that the move had come to nothing and to describe the 'military intelligentsia' (always a pejorative with him) as having lost the hearts of the masses, so encouraging the parties to hope for a comeback.[91]

This was a further factor, combining with his limited success in the Kokumin Dōmei and the labour movement, which helped to shift the focus of Nakano's effort away from domestic reform towards the international arena, with the further effect that his subsequent relations with the military tended to stress the latter field. To begin with, the central concern was with China, since Nakano discounted facile hopes among a section of the Establishment that Japan might benefit from new European dissensions. So in late 1935 he was supporting army-backed moves for autonomous regimes in North China and condemning the Nanking regime as an Anglo–American puppet working to suppress traditional local autonomy in the interests of compradors and imperialists. Before long, however, the Ethiopian war brought a new complexion to the world picture and greatly encouraged Nakano both by demonstrating the League of Nations' impotence and by suggesting how, with a dexterous use of air power, a less wealthy nation could checkmate the British navy.

His new outlook was heralded in a pamphlet published following his secession from the Kokumin Dōmei at the end of the year, entitled *Manifesto to the Japanese Poeple—through the smokescreen of the crisis in North China*. In the preface he writes:

I have constantly stood at the forefront of the political battle ... I now realise how many needless enemies I have made, for one projecting a bold design for the world with its basis in Japan. My perspectives are now abruptly altered. Now, as I transcend all of Japan's parties and factions, I have no enemies in terms of these. My only enemies are the stubbornness, the indecision, the indolence of society and I seek only to overcome these by summoning the vigour of a national resurgence.[92]

He was entering a phase in which Adachi is quoted as having said of him (no doubt alluding to his equestrian interests): 'Nakano is the wild horse of politics. We can't possibly keep a grip on his reins.'

4
Staking all on Japan's world mission

With his secession from the Kokumin Dōmei and the issue of his supra-party 'Manifesto to the Japanese People', Nakano entered the most controversial period of his career, lasting until the year before his death, which from the standpoint of his biographers presents both the greatest dramatic interest and the greatest difficulties for sympathetic treatment, in view of the disastrous outcome of policies he then advocated. During this time his key strategy was to ride the storm of the mounting world crisis and its repercussions in Japan, gambling on the prospect that the established structure would crumble under the stress of events and open the way to a reallocation of power in which he could effectively participate. It was therefore rather a time of action, improvised to meet rapid change, than of theorising, though he showed a good deal of resourcefulness in turning his stock of theory to account in meeting the demands of the moment. Only at the end of this period did he finally find it impossible to sustain a line that was both credible and distinctive.

One index of his shift of emphasis after 1935 from internal reorganisation to a focus on international strategy occurs in a Diet interpellation where, in contrast with his previous warning that industries based on armaments might lack adequate additional outlets, he now argued that such industries would find ready markets in adjacent countries and pointed out that the largest armament manufacturers were also the largest exporters.[93] He particularly cited Germany as having the right formula for a balance between strategic and consumer needs and accused anyone who suggested a clash between these (as he had once done) of 'alienating army and people', which would be fatal in a state of world crisis.

Parallel to his growing emphasis on global strategy as the key to internal reform, he placed increasing reliance on common action with the European Axis powers as representing the 'anti status quo camp' as against the international Establishment. This combination led in turn to a tendency for him to assimilate his political theory and action to Axis-inspired models. Although, since he had already rejected both liberalism and socialism, this did not entail any radical changes, it did tend to narrow his range of alternatives within the spectrum of Japanese politics. On the one hand, if offered the advantage that he could use the growing prestige of the Axis powers to counteract the influence that Anglo–Saxon models had long exercised over the minds of liberal intellectuals, as well as, though much less important, that of the Soviet Union over left wing reformists. But it also brought him into collision with the 'pure Japanist' or traditionalist Pan-Asian section of the right, to whom any alien ideology was a threat to the unique National Polity. He could therefore equally be attacked as 'fascist' by these elements, as well as liberals and leftists.

This term was already established in vernacular Japanese usage as a pejorative, in the sense of 'domineering' or 'high-handed'. Once, having had this epithet used against him and feeling it was hardly appropriate, he asked his sons whether they thought he was a fascist but they, accepting it in its popular sense, agreed that he was, rather taking him aback.[94] He himself, however, also sometimes used it almost as a pejorative, for example in replying to the charge of 'fascism' by claiming that it was the new bureaucrats who really provided a case of 'professional bureaucratic fascism'.[95]

The term first came to be commonly used of him through his confrontations with the Minseitō Diet member Saitō Takao, who was prominent as a critic of military intervention in politics. Saitō also decried the fashion of vague talk of national reform and reconstruction which, he said, was pursued by 'dropouts in the struggle for survival, political failures and half-baked scholars.' This may have sounded rather pointed to Nakano, who disposed of his argument as 'formalistic conservatism'. Nakano admitted, however, that the performance of senior military elements in the cause of social reform had been disappointing.

Referring to the condemnation of fascism by the National Polity wing he would argue, for instance:

> There are those who hold that nazism and fascism are incompatible with our national character but I believe that the human resolution to overcome adversity is at bottom in no way different whether in Germany, Italy or Japan.[96]

Again, he could try to clear up the 'misunderstanding' that fascism meant 'rule by violence' by defining it instead as meaning 'unity' and idealising it as strength grounded in justice and popular appeal—not an armchair theory but an 'empirical morality' evolved through struggle in the same spirit as Yōmeigaku.[97]

But he usually avoided this term in favour of others, sometimes his earlier 'strong politics' but normally an expression *zentaishugi* intended to be an equivalent of 'totalitarianism'. Since, however, his usage of it does not accord very explicitly with its European sense of a single-party dictatorship, it is perhaps best rendered more literally as 'totalism'. He had quickly dropped his use of the word 'dictatorship', probably as clashing too obviously with the National Polity credo that there must be no usurpation of the Emperor's prerogatives, nor any distinction of party or otherwise among his subjects in their capacity of 'assisting' him. The new term was convenient in that it could also be taken in the latter sense, as when Nakano contrasts totalism with sectionalism in the context of the 'family–state' principle, or speaks of a 'totalism unique to Japan'. He also evades too close a definition of the term in that 'it does not consist in laws, rules or organisation, but in relying on human initiative in guiding and applying it'.[98]

More often, however, in this period he uses it to imply something rather closer to the European conception, for example when speaking of the Tōhōkai as 'the nucleus of a national party which will one day take charge of Japanese politics'.[99] During the formation of the Imperial Rule Assistance Association, which marked his phase of greatest prominence in this period, he stood for a conception of that body as a national political entity which was not an indiscriminate combination of all groups. As always, he sought to develop the political expression of the lower classes as against the 'status quo forces' and now preferred to describe his movement as 'mass action' (*taishū undō*) implying a mobilisation of the underprivileged by 'renovationist' leadership.

In this respect, he claimed to represent a more authentic populism than could be attained by 'outmoded liberalism'.

> Fascism and nazism are quite distinct from the despotism of former days. They are not a conservative trend which has reverted to a pre-democratic stage. They are of a still more populist (*minshūteki*) character which has left democracy behind ... Totalism must transcend numbers and be based on essentials ... individuals being combined organically in common ideals and common sentiments.[100]

He could also say (bringing out his hopes regarding the role of crisis in stimulating reconstruction):

> We do not in the least yield to the democracies in respecting the liberty of the people as an element in the state structure but, in

that we are compelled to mobilise the upsurge of national feeling and attack problems at the root in the interests of swift and effective action, we are placed in the same situation as Germany and Italy.[101]

In a Diet speech he claims that totalism would solve the labour question by giving labour a voice in management, so that social democratic-style trade unions would no longer be necessary.

Thus, whereas in the preceding period Nakano had been largely concerned with attacking party liberalism and advocating his own conception of economic control, the decline of the parties left the way open for him to develop a new type of popular movement, now conversely protesting against the growth of economic control in a much more authoritarian form. This latter trend posed an alternative to Nakano's plans for meeting the crisis in that it amounted to the concentration of power in a narrowing section of the Establishment, in contrast with the recasting of the power structure that he hoped to achieve. He regularly called for the abolition of the Civil Service Appointment Ordinance in order to open the civil service to outside talent and portrayed the existing bureaucracy as stagnating in the absence of free competition, unbuffeted by the wild waves of society. He also naturally condemned the inversion of priorities presented by the subjection of the political process to administration, which should instead be governed by the political process.

In his struggle against the growing monopoly of power by high civil and military officials and privileged capital, he even adapted the theme of anti-semitism to the Japanese scene. Recalling Hitler's claim that Germany's defeat in the First World War had been due to Jewish domination of finance and administration in collusion with the German and Australian bureaucracy, he drew an analogy with the control of the wartime Japanese economy by bureaucrats and their capitalist collaborators in state-backed economic agencies.[102]. These, he would insist, were those who really had a 'Jewish mentality' (*yudayashugi*) and not, as sometimes charged by the new bureaucrats, the independent-minded industrialists who resisted the dead hand of bureaucratic control and were those really capable of directing Japan's crisis economy efficiently.

He also disparaged the 'pure Japanists' who in practice tended to support this power monopoly.

> What are called the right (*ukei*) are already unable to fulfil the hopes of the nation. They seek in mysticism a way out for their inadequate arguments and try to convey unintelligible aspects of that mysticism through the medium of classics that cannot be elucidated in contemporary language. Nothing of this kind can satisfy the national feelings of modern Japan.[103]

Although, he goes on to say, these rightists are described as 'fascists' (by liberals), 'it must be recognised that Hitler's movement is not a reactionary-revolutionary movement isolated from national feeling [as theirs is]'.

The image he himself tried to project certainly resembled his estimate of Hitler, whom he described as a simple 'patriot' (*shishi*) from the lower ranks of German society, which he was for that reason 'privileged' to represent. Similarly, 'it is our Tōhōkai that is entrusted with the privilege of guiding our society'.[104] He regarded Hitler's dedication as demonstrated by his celibacy and vegetarianism, just as Mussolini abstained from alcohol and tobacco, and, in a public relations handout prepared by his diplomatic adviser Nakayama Masaru for distribution on his visit to the Axis leaders in 1937–38, a similar note is struck. Nakano is described as a central figure in the renovationist movement, Japan's greatest orator, a true Japanese in faults and virtues, an economist of the school of Friedrich List (whom he had studied at Waseda and sometimes quoted, though not as a central authority) and a Confucian idealist who had been strengthened by tragedy and now lived 'the stoic life of a Zen monk'.[105]

During this period the administration did not take any very severe measures to suppress Nakano's activities, partly, no doubt, owing to his connections in the army and in big business and partly because he did not represent a problem as serious as the persistent threat of terrorism. But he was subjected to some harassment, particularly censorship. In three speeches published with the *Outline Plan*, for example, there are fourteen deletions, which are also quite marked in the book, *Go Straight Ahead!* (1938), reporting his visit to the Axis countries. Instances occur sporadically in his journalism over the following years, more especially as the war approached, when police interference with his meetings is also mentioned.

The global crisis: China, the Axis and the military

In his *Manifesto to the Japanese People* (1935), Nakano sought a basis for transcending party divisions in a united effort to cope with the crisis developing in North China. The Nanking regime had been widening its area of control by a program of currency unification financed by the British Reith–Ross Loans and this was being countered by the Japanese army in North China with the establishment of autonomous regimes, through which illicit trade was being promoted to undermine Nanking's control.

In his pamphlet, Nakano strongly commends the army for its efforts in contrast with the government's cautious attempts at compromise, represented especially by Finance Minister Takahashi, who was making every effort to play down the crisis and emphasise the limitations of Japan's strategic potential. Nakano enjoined faith in the robust characteristics of the Japanese race, who were no mere nation of 'cherry blossoms, geisha and dolls'. By a vigorous program of development on the continent, Japan would be able to withstand any blockade that might be imposed by the powers.

In the hope of initiating a high-level breakthrough, Nakano made a visit to China at the end of 1935, carrying a letter of introduction from Kita Ikki to the favourably disposed Foreign Minister Chang Ch'ün and apparently also going with the backing of Ishiwara.[106] Kita is said by this stage to have given up hopes of national reconstruction by coup in favour of a politically-based reorganisation centred on relations with China. Nakano was accompanied by his regular advisers and was able to interview Chiang Kai-shek early in the new year—not quite their first meeting.

When Chiang asked what he thought of the situation in the north, Nakano appealed for them not to 'argue like officials' about past rights and wrongs, but to transcend local frictions by entering into a grand offensive-defensive alliance and an economic union. Chiang seemed not unfavourable, saying that he realised he could not expect much real help from abroad in the event of an open clash with Japan, in which China would suffer huge losses. He warned, however, that this would provoke long term resistance which could only weaken both nations until they equally fell prey to the powers. They both were, he agreed, as interdependent as 'lips and teeth' and he hoped they could deal with each other in this realisation.[107]

On Nakano's return to Japan, he approached Foreign Minister Hirota and publicised the interview with Chiang in order to urge summit level action along these lines but these efforts were cut short by the 26 February insurrection. This event inspired Nakano's last flicker of hope that national reconstruction might be achieved before a deepening of international entanglements. According to Kita's testimony at his trial for involvement in the rising, he first heard of its occurrence in a telephone call from Nakano, who said: 'It looks as if something serious has started!'[108] Kita is elsewhere said to have told him not to take any rash action. On the same morning Nakano told his sons quite hopefully that a revolution had broken out and took them to see the rebel positions in the snow, saying, 'The sons of a samurai must get used to the sight of fires and battlegrounds.'

He was bitterly disappointed when the insurrection came to nothing and, on learning that Ishiwara, as a martial law administrator, had secured the rebels' flag bearing the legend 'Honour the Sovereign and Crush the Traitors!' and was keeping it in his office, he offered to buy it for ¥300 (one tenth of a Dietman's annual salary).[109] Later he used what influence he possessed in Prince Konoe's circle to have Kita's life spared and, in recognition of this, was presented after Kita's execution with a set of furniture left by him.

The army purge which followed the insurrection broke many of the links previously existing between army factions and civilian right wing bodies, weakening many of these. Besides, the restoration of the armed services' privilege of nominating their respective cabinet ministers enabled them to intervene more directly in the political process and decreased their need for allies. All this helped to divert Nakano from his earlier factional manoeuvres toward broader strategic issues. He wrote favourably of War Minister Terauchi's role in dictating the composition of the succeeding Hirota cabinet, as he regarded this action as at least averting the complete domination by 'status quo forces' that would have resulted from Hirota's plan to appoint Yoshida Shigeru, of the pro-British foreign ministry faction, foreign minister and cabinet organiser.[110] Even so, Nakano described the new government as a phase of stalemate between old and new forces, making the pun that Hirota had merely 'picked up' (*'hirotta'*) power, rather than achieving it through merit.

Nakano did, however, still sometimes express reservations about this kind of army dominance. He commended Hitler for his ability to control the military in the case of the seizure of the Rhineland, which was carried out successfully against his generals' objections, owing to Hitler's wider grasp of the situation. He also complained of the 'military intelligentsia's' willingness to back the new bureaucrats' plans for state management of the economy. An important instance was the Electric Power Bill now being proposed, though this was for a time to be shelved owing to opposition from operators in this field, who included some of Nakano's closest backers.

Late in the year Nakano visited Manchuria and the East Hopei Autonomous Region, following this up with an article 'Sino–Japanese Problems in 1936'.[111] He had not been satisfied with the situation as he had found it and wrote that the real 'double diplomacy' was not the discrepancy between army and foreign ministry policies—the usual sense—but the shameless contrast between Japan's bullying of China and its craven truckling to Britain and the United States, a combination which both drove and encouraged the Chinese to seek support from the latter.

Yet the habitual ambiguity of his attitudes to China was again revealed the following year on the outbreak of the China Incident when, by a slight shift in this argument, he reasoned that blows struck against the new United front of Kuomintang and Communists were in reality directed against the Anglo–American and Soviet plotters who were manipulating them.[112] When Prince Konoe, as Prime Minister, spoke of his hopes of localising the conflict, Nakano, as on the outbreak of the Manchurian Incident, argued that a unilateral undertaking of restraint was meaningless and dangerous if the other side retained freedom of action. He also commented, significantly for his whole political strategy in this period, that the struggle would not impede Japan's development but rather spur it on.

It is worth noting that Nakano's former colleague and rival in oratory, Nagai Ryūtarō, then a cabinet minister, was also distinguished by a warlike stand both now and subsequently—so continuing the striking parallel in their evolution, the chief difference being that Nagai continued to operate securely within the ruling circles, while Nakano was at best on their outer fringes.

In September 1937 the Tōhōkai held a general conference to press for the vigorous prosecution of the China campaign in order to prevent the development of a situation of the type seen in the Spanish Civil War. In an article warning of this possibility, Nakano dismissed Chiang's prediction in their interview of the effects of a long term conflict by denying that the Kuomintang could rally the Chinese people to maintain a resistance like that of the Spartans against Persia or of Japan against the Mongols, because it was a mere puppet of 'alien forces' and a purely regional power based on the Lower Yangtse comprador community.[113]

At the same time, he could hardly help recognising that the conflict had made the prospect of any ultimate Sino-Japanese solidarity extremely doubtful and, with this disadvantage, Japan could hardly maintain a strong front against the Western powers without backing from elsewhere, which could now only come from the Axis. Nakano had been obliged for the time being, uniquely in his career, to lay aside his usual hopes for an understanding with the Soviet Union, admitting the dangers posed by the eastward spread of Soviet industrialisation and conceding that hopes for any collaboration were ruled out by Stalin's new posture of courting the Western democracies in an anti-fascist front. This question led him to express some doubts on the conclusion of the Anti-Comintern Pact, complaining that, though intended as a means of coping with the current international crisis, it could intensify it further.[114]

He now, however, adopted the role of an apostle of closer Axis ties as the key to directing the East Asian crisis in a favourable direction and thereby also changing the domestic power structure by discrediting pro-Anglo–Saxon elements in the bureaucracy, as well as suggesting alternative models of economic planning to the 'crypto-socialist' methods of the new bureaucrats. He therefore decided to visit the

Axis leaders as a 'national envoy', in contrast to the regular diplomats representing the 'status quo'. To give him suitable credentials, the Tōhōkai held a mass rally on 11 November 1937, attended, among other publicly known figures, by the 'Three Great Elders' Miyake, Tōyama and Tokutomi Sohō. Nakano was drawing close to Tokutomi for the first time after long distrusting him for supporting the old clan oligarchs. The rally was followed by a procession of 3000 supporters, bearing Axis flags and large Tōhōkai lanterns, past the palace to Tokyo railway station. Further rallies were held in other cities further west along Nakano's route.

In Rome, he easily obtained an interview with Mussolini and his Foreign Minister Count Ciano, which the Japanese embassy wished to limit to ten minutes of courtesies; but Nakano claims to have caught his hosts' interest by forthrightly criticising the regular diplomats who had denied any Japanese intention to take Nanking—a claim now falsified by events. He went on to say that the Japanese people, being now aroused, would never let the government compromise in China and added that though the Manchurian Incident, the killing of Inukai and the February Insurrection might look like the onset of chaos, each of these episodes had improved the situation in Japan.

After an hour's interview, Mussolini authorised Nakano to convey his willingness to enter into a comprehensive alliance with Japan and had him take down a message to Japanese youth saying: 'March straight ahead—straight ahead! If you encounter obstacles, keep marching straight ahead!'[115] Nakano used this phrase as the title of his account of the trip.

It proved more difficult to arrange an interview with Hitler. The reason Nakano gives was that Hitler had been disgusted at the irresponsibility of Japanese diplomats. With the help of the strongly pro-German military attache Ōshima, however, he met Foreign Minister Baron Neurath and other leading nazis and, finally, Hitler himself.

Here again the Japanese embassy tried to restrict the interview but Hitler prolonged it to 50 minutes. In the course of their conversation, Hitler denied any territorial claims in East Asia, hoping only for trade opportunities, to which the Comintern was the main obstacle. He looked to Japan to rectify this problem but hoped that the war would not be too exhausting. At this Nakano assured him that the real fight was already over. The Kuomintang was now merely a regional force and if the Japanese were compelled to keep order over most of the country they would favour nations which 'understood the situation'.

Nakano later described Hitler as much more cautious and deliberate in discussion than Mussolini, who always had ready answers.

On hearing his account of them, Tōyama remarked that Hitler reminded him of Saigō and Mussolini of Katsu Awa—that most agile representative of the shogunate in its last days.

Back in Japan, after reporting personally to Konoe, who had given him an unpublicised letter of introduction to the Axis leaders, Nakano addressed meetings of the army and navy headquarters staffs, at which he not only advocated a military alliance with the Axis but urged the capture of Canton as the last measure needed to isolate the Kuomintang and defy Britain. Ishiwara is said to have bemoaned the spiritlessness of the headquarters officers in calmly listening while Nakano 'shamelessly expounded his amateur strategy'.[116]

This marked a major breach between the two, since Ishiwara had done his utmost to restrain military action in China in order to prepare for the clash with the Soviet Union which came first in his strategy for Armageddon. Ishiwara, however, soon found himself excluded from influence in army mainstream circles, earning especially the hostility of Tōjō, who was heavily committed to the China adventure.

Despite the falsification of Nakano's early optimism on China, he continued to press for reckless measures there, such as the exercise of belligerent rights against nations abetting resistance to Japan. Another suggestion was the seizure of foreign concessions, perhaps after a *fait accompli* by Chinese and Japanese youth volunteers, upon which they could be transferred to a friendly Chinese regime. He was suspicious of peace moves through Wang Ching-wei, who he suggested might be a British or French agent, and preferred to work through the local regimes already established by the army. It was only in mid-1940 that he spoke clearly in favour of Wang's regime, defending it against the Anglo-American charge of being a puppet government and describing it as the nucleus of the future 'East Asia League', which was Ishiwara's favourite theme.[117]

As the corollary to his China policy, Nakano naturally supported the growing army pressure for a full military alliance with the Axis, at the same time arguing that the campaign should not be left to the army but be backed by a national movement. The patriotic societies were also threatening terror against members of the 1939 Hiranuma Cabinet resisting the conclusion of a full alliance, notably the foreign and navy ministers. When these negotiations and the cabinet itself collapsed on the conclusion of the Nazi–Soviet Non-aggression Pact, both the army and the patriotic societies were badly deflated but Nakano was encouraged to revive long-held hopes of an understanding with the Soviet Union as well as the Axis, which would allow Japan's full effort to be directed against the colonial powers in China and Southern Asia. He had viewed the border clashes between

Japanese and Soviet forces as evidence of collusion between the Russians and Western powers and now rightly predicted that these clashes would cease. He defended Hitler against right wing charges of treachery by arguing that he had been driven to this step by the dilatoriness and double dealing of the Hiranuma cabinet and he looked forward to a future opportunity to conclude both an alliance with the Axis and a non-aggression pact with the Soviet Union.[118] Although the succeeding Abe and Yonai cabinets were unfavourable to such suggestions, both these hopes were realised under the Second Konoe Cabinet in the wake of the German military successes of mid-1940.

To Nakano, this development was especially welcome as opening a way out from the impasse in China. He had already conceded that the Kuomintang did command a national movement there,[119] as grounds for summoning a comparable national effort in Japan to confront it. Now the prospect arose of solving the China question by recasting the strategic picture with a 'southern advance' against Britain and the other colonial powers, enjoying the support of the Axis and the non-intervention of the Soviet Union—even, perhaps, of the United States.

Development of the Tōhōkai

The activities of the Tōhōkai tended on the whole to be governed by international issues of the kind just discussed, though some concern with social issues and domestic policies was maintained and sometimes emphasised when the situation warranted. Nakano's group of seceders from the Kokumin Dōmei in the Diet faced their first independent election in February 1936, having had little time to prepare for it. Some of them described their affiliation as Yūkōkai, this having originally been the name of Nakano's constituency organisation. Nine of them gained election, as against only five of Adachi's group. The Seiyūkai, campaigning on an anti-bureaucratic line, lost heavily, while the pro-government Minseitō was more successful and the Shakai Taishūtō (Social Masses Party) emerged to prominence with eighteen seats.

In mid-year Nakano's Diet colleagues were formally affiliated to the Tōhōkai, which was accordingly declared a political association, though it retained a distinction from conventional parties by avoiding any very tight organisation. On this occasion the journal *Gakan* was renamed *Tōtairiku* (Eastern Continent) and in the May issue from which this took effect Miyake inserted an editorial note saying that the new name alluded to the need to correct the anomalous situation where the more numerous peoples of the Eastern Continent were oppressed by the less numerous inhabitants of the Western Continent.

In the following months the Tōhōkai was chiefly occupied with agitation for rural reform, including such activities as collecting signatures on petitions for rural debt liquidation. In the process it built up a network of Farmer's Leagues (*Nōmin Remmei*) which remained an important wing of the movement and contributed to the election of Tōhōkai candidates in prefectural assemblies

In this period a number of right-wing renovationist groups, conscious of their weakness in the aftermath of the February Insurrection, projected the formation of a February Society as a basis for common action and approached Nakano with the proposal that the Tōhōkai participate in it. Although its proponents were willing to accord him a leading role in the society, Nakano refused to contemplate any other course than that all the other groups join the Tōhōkai outright. This they were unwilling to do and the plan proved abortive.[120]

The Tōhōkai fought its first general election as a party in 1937, when General Hayashi as prime minister called a sudden dissolution in the hope of building a stronger Diet base—a plan that misfired. The Tōhōkai made progress, gaining twelve seats, while the Shakai Taishūtō rose dramatically to 37. The Tōhōkai platform adopted for this election remained its basic statement of policy and read as follows:

1 In recognition of Japan's international environment, rapid progress will be ensured in developing resources and nurturing national power.
2 National defence in the broad sense will be undertaken by political action, allowing the armed forces to concentrate on defence in the narrow sense.
3 With a view to the rapid expansion and improvement of productive power, economic controls will be developed along the correct lines.
4 Class privilege and class struggle will be eliminated in accordance with the principles of totalism.
5 The livelihood of farmers, workers and medium and small entrepreneurs will be guaranteed, so cultivating the sources of national vitality.[121]

This platform marks the adoption of the term 'totalism' as Nakano's watchword. It also reflects his reservations about wholesale army domination in politics, or at least a desire not to be regarded as a mere apologist for the army. The third plank was defined as countering 'the transformation of Japanese industry into a bureaucratic capitalism through outmoded socialistic thought, centred on the bill for private ownership and state management of electric power'. This was one issue on which Nakano's stand, as well as that of his backers, did not follow the line of the military planners.

The party consolidated its image by a general conference at a new headquarters, also in Akasaka. Still maintaining the distinction from conventional parties (being rather a 'nucleus for national renovation'), it named no president, Nakano's formal post being head of the External Relations Section, though he is also referred to as 'chairman'. His address to the conference was optimistic and he interpreted the Shakai Taishūtō gains as a sign that the decline of the established parties would be succeeded by a phase of socialism but that, when its faults were exposed in turn, 'our advance will come'.[122]

Following the Hayashi cabinet's fiasco, Prince Konoe's first cabinet was formed in June 1937 and Nakano was disappointed in hopes he had come to entertain of obtaining a seat in it. Like so many others, he had been cultivating Konoe in the expectation that he would become the pivotal figure in the political scene. Nakano's approach to him had been associated with Ishiwara's plan for strategic industries, in which Ikeda Seihin of Mitsui had shown interest. Konoe was the only prime minister of the prewar decade of whom Nakano wrote in any way favourably—also being in the habit of speaking proudly at home of 'Konoe-san's' interest in his ideas. One reason suggested for his exclusion from the cabinet was his apparent commitment to the mainstream element in the army, which Konoe wished to restrain.

Kazami, on the other hand, became cabinet secretary, which would have meant an intensification of Nakano's disappointment, since this old friend and loyal associate had now for the first time outstripped him. Nakano commented on this cabinet that it was premature and would have been better formed a little later when the political stalemate was more obvious.[123]

This was probably one reason why Nakano tried to make so much political capital out of the China Incident, which broke out in July 1937. The Tōkōkai, holding a rally to press for resolute action, went on record as supporting a 'China Punitive Movement'. Carried along by its warlike impetus, the Tōkōkai joined the Shakai Taishūtō in strong support for the National General Mobilisation Law which provided the legal basis for wartime controls, as well as the Electric Power Control Law, now revived and passed. While the Shakai Taishūtō frankly supported these measures as a step towards state socialism, the Tōhōkai lacked such a clear basis in principle and Nakano qualified his stand by warning that neither measure would be effective 'without popular support and the capacity to mobilise the talents of all, both in and out of office'.[124]

On his return from Europe, he concentrated on building up a mass movement modelled on the Nazi Party as he represented it, having at its core a youth movement called from late 1938 the Orient Youth Corps (*Tōhō Seinentai*). Its members wore a uniform of a black field cap, a deep navy-blue shirt, a dark red tie and an armband with a swastika-like device based on the initial character for 'Tōhōkai', meaning 'East'.

About this time, the problems Konoe had experienced from army interference in peace manoeuvres and other matters prompted him to explore the possibilities of forming an independent national political organisation to restrain the army. Among his associates, however, a division was early apparent between a social reformist group, represented by Arima Yoriyasu, who favoured the encouragement of popular initiative, and others more authoritarian, such as Home Minister Suetsugu Nobumasa, who thought in terms of the use of public funds and the appointment of prefectural governors as branch heads. Nakano observed that such features would make the new body a mere extension of the National Spiritual Mobilisation Movement,[125] which he habitually derided as mere 'drill', and naturally could not favour in that it represented a bureaucratically directed 'mass movement' directly competing with his own.

He tried to seize the initiative in the reshaping of politics by calling the First National Congress of the Tōhōkai in January 1939, in an address to which he described Konoe as a brilliant individual, but as being sundered from the masses in 'the bath-houses, cafes, working-class suburbs and villages', so lacking in vitality, like a 'daffodil cut from the stem'.[126] By merging with the masses, however, the Tōhōkai would provide a sound base for future leadership.

Soon afterwards, Nakano made a bid to widen his base by a merger with the Shakai Taishūtō. Although this seemed to many to be an improbable matching of the extreme right and left wings of Diet politics, the two parties as already noted had taken similar stands on many issues through their support of army interests. Some elements of the Shakai Taishūtō had also come over to the Tōhōkai as a result of the police crackdown in the 'Popular Front Cases' of late 1937 to early 1938—this being the Japanese authorities' reply to the Comintern's current policy of forming a broad 'popular front' among diverse left-wing or anti-fascist elements. In the eyes of many of that party's leadership too, the best alternative to the 'popular front' would be a 'national front' beginning with a merger with the Tōhōkai. The Tōhōkai also hoped that the move would secure its link with the Farmers' Leagues, which were restive.

The first contact was made between Nakano and a leader of the other party who was, as in so many such cases, a fellow native of

Fukuoka—upon which the Kokumin Dōmei was also approached. Though Adachi was at first favourable, 'provided the Shakai Taishūtō had given up its class character', he was dissuaded from taking part by Diet groups working on a different plan for interparty amalgamation, in which Nagai was especially active.

Nakano therefore decided to proceed without him and lost no time in drafting a joint declaration, which he presented at the sickbed of the other party's executive committee chairman, Abe Isoo. As Abe agreed to the statement, though with reservations about his own participation, it was made public at once.

Although brief, it was dramatic in content, speaking of fulfilling Japan's mission in East Asia through a return to the principle of 'service by the whole people', which underlay Japan's National Polity, admitting no 'policies of privilege, clique, class or self-righteousness'. The two parties, it said, whatever their past differences, were one in solicitude for nation and people and, in the true 'Japanese spirit' (*Yamatodamashii*), looked to sympathisers from all quarters to join in establishing a totalistic national party, for which a preparatory committee would now be set up.[127]

The preparatory committee began its activities with a banquet serving wild boar stew supplied by Kumamoto members, at which addresses were given by Tokutomi, Miyake, the Shakai Taishūtō's secretary-general Asō Hisashi and Nakano. Tōyama, the third Great Elder, was dissuaded from participating by associates in the Pure Japanist camp, such as the Great Japan Production Party and the Kokuryūkai, who accused Nakano of aiming at a 'Western-style totalitarian single national party'.[128] For some time, therefore, Nakano and Tōyama were again divided by this kind of conflict.

The committee made some progress, choosing the name Kakushin Shintō (New Renovationist Party), drawing up a platform and fixing the date for an inaugural meeting. The platform read:

1 In accordance with the basic principle of the nation's foundation, the national spirit of the Japanese people will be enhanced, contributing to the development of world culture.
2 A new economic structure will be established with the reform of capitalism and a basis in the common public interest.
3 The New Order in East Asia will be established and international relations reorganised.[129]

Arima's and Kazami's Japan Reformist Rural Council agreed to join the party but rival tacticians, especially Nagai, set about undermining it among less committed elements in the Shakai Taishūtō. The resulting tensions came to a head over the question of the new party's chief office-bearers. The Shakai Taishūtō expected one of its leaders to be given the top position in view of its larger Diet membership, but the Tōhōkai considered that, as the basic principle was totalism and the Shakai Taishūtō was joining as a group of 'recanters' (*tenkōha*) from socialism, Nakano should be top man.

This was the same sort of problem that had aborted the formation of a February Society as a basis for right wing renovationist unity in 1936. A variety of titles and structures was put forward in a search for compromise but a combined meeting of the leadership convinced them that the time was not yet ripe, as they put it in a joint announcement. This added that friendly relations would be maintained with a view to future opportunities but Nakano now wrote to Abe in terms that ruled these out. He seems to have recoiled from this whole course of action and felt that the experience had quenched his last spark of hope in Diet-centred manoeuvres. He is quoted as saying: 'I have formed the decision to make a direct appeal to Japan's crisis awareness and to struggle for the establishment of an Imperial Way totalistic party'. In a review of the episode, he wrote that a basic difference in strategy had also emerged, as the Shakai Taishūtō had hoped to proceed with a series of mergers with other parties, while Nakano saw a need to maintain a clear distinction from the established parties as such.[130] The platform framed for the new party was adopted as the Tōhōkai's own.

A matter of days later Nakano set out on a visit to the China front with War Minister Itagaki's approval, doubtless to divert attention from the merger fiasco. On the way, however, still very agitated, he spoke strongly in a press interview about politics being in 'a state of paralysis'. Because of this and his sudden departure while the Diet was in session, moves began among the two major parties for his expulsion from the Diet. His own Diet support was quickly eroded in the wake of the merger fiasco and ultimately only four members, led by Mitamura, remained affiliated to the party. Much of this falling away is attributed to Nakano's excessive admiration for Hitler, his close identification with the army line and his generally dictatorial attitudes—features which many of his party had hoped would be mitigated by the merger.

On his return to Japan he found that he had no option other than to resign from the Diet. He rejected any suggestion that he might apologise. In a public statement he said:

> The recent failure was my final disillusionment about a new party projected to centre on Diet members and I take full responsibility for it. Considering these circumstances, I now resolve to resign from the Diet and to hurl myself naked into the midst of the nation's masses.[131]

His constituency organisation in Fukuoka continued to function under his brother Taisuke, who had assumed full-time party work after failing in business. Political representations were processed by the remaining Tōhōkai Diet members. Meanwhile, Prince Konoe's known wish to develop a broader political base offered the prospect that, if Nakano could contribute something towards this, he should be assured of a place in an altered power structure.

The new intensive phase of his mass movement was stimulated by an increase in international tensions, including clashes with the British in Tientsin and with the Soviet Union at Nomonhan. Nakano also began to shift his emphasis away from the deadlocked China situation to what seemed the more hopeful line of the Southern Advance. He was encouraged in this by his important backer Tsuda Shingo of Kanebō, a leading advocate of the seizure of Singapore while, as a military adviser, General Itagaki was optimistic about United States neutrality. The new campaign was therefore begun in June 1939, with an anti-British Rally of East Asian Peoples', attended by Indonesian, Middle Eastern, Filipino and Indian representatives. This was followed up by an energetic nationwide campaign which built up a grassroots organisation on a scale little known in Japan, where parties have usually consisted only of Diet members and electoral organisations.

The rapid growth of Tōhōkai membership over the next year or so brought organisational problems. A party directive issued in early 1940 emphasised the recruitment of a cadre among younger 'renovationist' elements in economic and social organisations, especially employees, intellectuals and returned servicemen.[132] A regular source of support arose from elements of the Shakai Taishūtō who were dissatisfied with that party's tendency to identify its aims with those of the 'control bureaucrats'. In this way Nakano increased his following among the urban and rural proletariat but since this came at a time when the morale of this sector of society was being shattered by police suppression and conservative 'spiritual mobilisation' propaganda, the core of the Tōhōkai's drive and thinking was securely located in the less privileged sectors of the commercial class, those closest to Nakano's own social background.

Data based on police sources show membership totals of 7037 (mostly Farmers' Leagues) at the end of 1937; at the end of 1938, 10 296 in Tokyo and nine prefectural branches; and 22 742 (plus 3252 in youth groups) in Tokyo and 31 prefectural branches in March 1941[133] when the party was re-established after a period as a cultural organisation during Nakano's participation in the Imperial Rule Assistance Association. Local branches, each with its own flag for ceremonial purposes, numbered over 100, while members were described as 'comrades' (*dōshi*) rather than by any more formalised term, so that the criteria of membership were rather loose.[134] A trial was made of financing the mass movement by charging 15 *sen* per head admission to meetings for covering costs and, as attendances did not diminish, this was raised to 30 *sen*. The Youth Corps also contributed ¥2 per annum for use in producing pamphlets to sell at 30 *sen* each.

The Tōhōkai was naturally not in favour with the authorities under the Abe and Yonai cabinets, which tried to conciliate the United States and Britain, partly in reaction against the Nazi–Soviet Pact and partly in an attempt to adjust trade relations with the United States after that country's discontinuance of the Treaty of Commerce. But a major change occurred in mid-1940 when the army, encouraged by Axis military successes in Europe, overthrew the Yonai cabinet to make way for the Tripartite Alliance, which was soon concluded by the succeeding Second Konoe Cabinet.

Overnight, Nakano came to seem like a prophet whose faith in the Axis had now been justified by events. He was therefore accorded an important role in the next major political development in Japan—the creation of the Imperial Rule Assistance Association, designed as the overall political and social framework for Japan's wartime order.

Participation in the early IRAA

The formative period of the IRAA was undoubtedly the most complex episode in modern Japanese history, as the disintegration of the previous political process precipitated a kaleidoscopic struggle among innumerable factions to attain the highest possible standing in the projected 'New Structure'. Four main streams can be traced in the flood of embattled cliques. First, remnants of the older parties hoped for a major regrouping that would restore their influence—to some extent still in association with big business, but rather less so since Zaibatsu interests had come to secure direct representation on cabinet seats responsible for economic policy. Second, reformist intellectuals like Arima and Kazami (now justice minister), centred on Konoe's brain trust and with some popular following, were more concerned with broad social reconstruction. Third, the mainstream in the army aimed at achieving the maximum concentration of political power in the interests of the National Defence State, on the one hand maintaining links with the new bureaucrats and on the other with extremist politicians seeking 'national renovation' through a single national party. Fourth, the 'pure Japanist' or patriotic societies, associated with Hiranuma's machine, the Imperial Way faction of the army and the reservists, saw their main duty as lying in the prevention of any change to the National Polity by the other groups, which they warned would result in a new shogunate, in nazi or crypto-communist guise. They therefore tended to cooperate with the home ministry bureaucrats to preserve the administrative structure and with the Zaibatsu, where these felt threatened by plans for drastic economic reorganisation. Ideological conflict polarised between political elements in the third group (notably Nakano), now described as the 'renovationist (or radical) right' (*kakushin uyoku*), and those of the fourth, known as the 'ideological (or traditionalist) right' (*kannen uyoku*), in which Tōyama was prominent. The Genyōsha itself was little in evidence, having now become a purely local body with mainly educational interests.

As the New Structure Movement gained momentum with the self-dissolution of the parties from mid-1940, the Tōhōkai joined a federation called the Tōa Kensetsu Kokumin Remmei (National League for the Construction of East Asia), led by Admiral Suetsugu and including Hashimoto Kingorō's Greater Japan Youth Party and the Kokumin Dōmei.[135] Nakano wrote to Konoe just before the fall of the Yonai cabinet suggesting that, as an indiscriminate amalgamation of all bodies could achieve nothing worthwhile, the primary initiative in reorganisation could best be left to Suetsugu, Adachi, Hashimoto and himself.[136] In a public statement, while freely using Restorationist slogans like 'Unity of Sovereign and People' and Eight Corners under One Roof', he outlined his plan for the movement's development through four phases: formation of the party nucleus, national reorganisation, political and administrative reform and, lastly, economic reform under an Economic General Staff.[137]

Among the plethora of plans submitted to Konoe, the League contributed one, representing a consensus among its leaders, which proposed a Supreme National Political Committee combining government and Supreme Command, the filling of cabinet posts by the leaders of the national party organisation and a system of multi-tiered electorates. To this would be added a 'cooperative industrial structure' along the lines of Nakano's *Outline Plan*.[138]

The rival National Polity grouping at the same time formed a comprehensive 'Council for Meeting the Situation' (*Jikyoku Kyōgikai*) and submitted a counter-proposal calling for a purely spiritual reform. Konoe's leaning was rather towards the latter side, especially as one of his aims was to counter the army mainstream by rallying Imperial Way influence in the army and elsewhere. A close associate also suggests that he was intimidated by threats of terror from the National Polity wing, as well as hurt by their accusations of plotting a new shogunate.[139] Thus, although Nakano, Hashimoto and Suetsugu were all included in the New Structure Preparatory Committee called to hammer out practical proposals, the traditionalist right were given equal representation while Konoe in his speech opening their deliberations insisted that there must be no monopoly of power by a 'restored shogunate, using the Emperor as an organ'. All groups of political significance were represented on the Committee, which also included Ogata (for the Press) and Nagai, as well as Arima, who chaired most of its meetings and later became the first director-general of the Imperial Rule Assistance Association.

During the six committee sessions, sharp differences occurred over the proposed organisation's status, as the Military Affairs Bureau chief, General Mutō Akira (then the army's main political agent) frankly called for a single national party structure. This challenge was only overcome by a cabinet threat to resign. The proposed body was therefore ruled to be not a political association, which would imply the exclusion of some part of the nation, but a body 'complementary to the government'. The prime minister would therefore be its president *ex officio*. Another question hotly debated was whether the branch heads should be prefectural governors—one crucial for the body's character as administrative or political. The Committee being deadlocked, this was provisionally left to the president's discretion. The compromise name 'Imperial Rule Assistance Association' was suggested by Ogata.

In a rally, held just before the IRAA's inauguration, to celebrate the Tripartite Alliance, Nakano said that a movement like the New Structure was only possible because, owing to Japan's unique National Polity, even opposing groups could combine. But he attacked the suggestion that branches should be headed by governors. If the IRAA were used only as an instrument of bureaucratic control, he warned, the people would not identify with it and would feel no shame in black-marketing or other anti-social practices. Besides, to the extent that the people were effectively regimented, they would become so passive that they would be easy for a conqueror to take over, as France had proved to be.[140] He was at least right, regarding this last point, in predicting the smoothness of the postwar Occupation, which was quite probably due to reasons of this sort.

Nakano was appointed one of the eleven executive directors of the IRAA—along with Hashimoto and Nagai—and converted the Tōhō-kai into a cultural organisation named the Shintōsha, after Kaneko's former academy in Dairen. Among its affiliates was an academy, called the Shintōjuku, for the practice of the martial arts and studies in thought and history, where Nakano sometimes lectured. Kaneko had been very much in his thoughts recently, probably from speculating on how he would have faced the present situation, and from this time on Nakano displayed a piece of calligraphy by Kaneko in his guest room.

Nakano divided most of his time between meetings of the IRAA Board of Directors, which was to advise the government on policy and national attitudes, and speaking tours ostensibly meant to heighten popular involvement in the IRAA but naturally tending to increase the specific weight of his own faction within it. Hashimoto, who had also reorganised his Youth Party as the Sekiseikai (Loyalty Society) was similarly active. The traditionalist right bitterly resented the influence of the radical right in the IRAA due to its much greater membership numbers and Akao Bin, now one of the leading figures in the Japanist wing, accused its rivals of insincerity for not dissolving their own organisations entirely. A serious assault on Nakano's touring party during a visit to Hiroshima in February 1941, when his youth leader was badly stabbed, is attributed to the traditionalist right. It is of some interest that Nakano's one-time 'bodyguard', Terada Inejirō, was now in the rival camp but his former function was from this time taken over by Satō Morio, an ex-soldier from the China front and later one of Nakano's most loyal biographers.

The issue most responsible for bringing tensions in the IRAA to a head was the plan drawn up by the Kikakuin (Planning Board) for the Economic New Structure. This represented an extreme form of state control, involving the 'freeing of management from capitalistic restraints applied to the pursuit of profit'. This was to be achieved by limiting dividends and by the public control of top managerial appointments in key industries or control agencies, these being co-ordinated by the IRAA Planning Bureau. Smaller enterprises would be ruthlessly rationalised.[141]

As the plan's contents became known it was bitterly attacked both by business and by the traditionalist right, a leading group of which, including Tōyama and Araki, wrote to Konoe demanding the dismissal of socialists in the IRAA. Some of the same group issued a 'Manifesto in Defence of the Constitution', pointing out that the Constitution protected private property and accusing the 'renovationists' of aiding the enemy by sowing dissension.

In cabinet discussion in December 1940 the plan was attacked and amended by ex-party and financial ministers, with some resistance to this by the armed services. It was then submitted to the IRAA Board of Directors, which tended to favour the original Kikakuin plan. Nakano, having ties with both business and the military, tried to work out an alternative which might better serve the ends of both. In the Board, he presented a nine-point statement of 'basic principles for economic reform', which attacked the Kikakuin for 'shallow theorising' and 'left wing totalism disguised as Imperial Way totalism', 'not considering the practical operation of private organisations but, in the name of a uniform pattern of private ownership and public management, calling for their amalgamation into national policy companies'. As against this he proposed a role for 'private bodies as agencies of national policy in their own right', allowing a measure of competition between them in the interests of efficiency.[142] He saw France under Popular Front socialism as the disastrous example, while Nazi Germany had found the right formula.

He took some part in the formulation of a compromise plan for an Industrial Organisations Bill, which would provide for economic control through autonomous associations along lines sketched in his *Outline Plan*. These would select leaders to collaborate with the Kikakuin for planning and with the ministry of commerce and industry for implementing projects, these being executed by instructions from the government to the associations.[143]

Other features were that excess profits would be converted to bonds; smaller enterprises would be rationalised only when in difficulties; salaries would be proportional to efficiency and management would not be subject to public appointment, except in the case of the industrial associations and then on the basis of nomination by members.

Although this Bill was scheduled for debate in the Diet, the government was experiencing such difficulties there that it was decided instead to develop the planning system by decree under the General Mobilisation Law. Nakano described the Bill as having been suppressed by 'hypocritical bureaucrats and Diet members serving liberalistic capitalists'. Owing to the resulting pattern of direct confrontation between government and big business, political intervention of the kind Nakano had hoped to exercise was ruled out, so that he had little to offer business interests for their support, of which there is much less sign from this time.

The government's problems in the Diet centred on attacks on the IRAA as unconstitutional. One argument was that the Diet lost its independence in legislation and review if all members belonged to a body headed by the prime minister. At this time, Nakano's lack of a Diet seat deprived him of any opportunity to defend the IRAA in the Lower House. Diet members moved to cut the IRAA's budget, while the Zaibatsu collaborated by withholding interim funds on the grounds of alleged 'red' influence within it. To control the situation, Konoe brought Hiranuma into the cabinet as home minister, while Kazami as justice minister was replaced by General Yanagawa of the Imperial Way faction.

Upon Hiranuma's declaring in the Diet that the IRAA had no political status, being only an official agency, and promising to reorganise it appropriately, its budget was passed but Nakano and Hashimoto promptly resigned from it. Nakano wrote that the IRAA, for the price of a budget, was 'being butchered by outmoded forces, professional rightists, finance capitalists and fifth columnists'.[144]

Although General Mutō still tried to preserve a political role for the IRAA, Arima and the whole headquarters staff were obliged to resign within a month, the Executive Director system being abolished and the whole organisation taken over by home ministry bureaucrats, with prefectural governors as branch heads. Thus the army did not attain clear political dominance until the formation of the Tōjō cabinet, it being also only then that the system of economic control associations was finalised under Kishi Nobusuke as minister for commerce and industry.

Meanwhile the leader of the Kokuryūkai, Kuzuu Yoshihisa, expressed satisfaction with the outcome of the IRAA struggle, saying that, at least, 'party men were better than reds'.[145] He and other traditionalist rightists were, however, dissatisfied with the appointment of the agile Nagai to head the IRAA's new East Asia Bureau, as he was too suggestive of the 'status quo'. Suetsugu also retained a leading role after the reorganisation.

Into the Pacific War—retreat to Restorationism

In a statement issued on leaving the IRAA, Nakano declared that as all channels of political action in the proper sense had now ceased functioning, society was sinking into a morass of intrigue and that the Tōhōkai would be revived to cope with this situation. There was no legal obstacle to this because the earlier parties had dissolved themselves in a race to share in the new power structure, rather than from any compulsion. Besides, as the IRAA was now declared non-political, a political Tōhōkai could not be regarded as competing with it.

Nakano was now formally described as president of the party, whose new platform read as follows:

1   Conveying to those above the loyalty of the masses, we will, in accordance with the provisions of the Constitution, take the lead in manifesting the Imperial Way in politics.
2   The pure spirit of Japan will be enhanced, invigorating Greater East Asia and proclaiming justice throughout the world.

3 An economic order of service by the whole people will be established, demanding labour and sacrifice from the whole nation but promising honour and livelihood.[146]

The rhetoric adopted was clearly meant to smooth over some recent animosities but as the late convulsions had left Nakano with reduced political leverage, he was obliged to take a more reckless line than ever, gambling on the effectiveness of playing on two major sources of tension—the hardships suffered by smaller enterprises under intensifying economic controls and the hysteria aroused by the headlong drive towards war. For the time being, Nakano concentrated more on the latter.

He had remained a prominent spokesman for the Southern Advance throughout his spell in the IRAA. The fall of Holland and France to German arms had made the proposal more feasible and he described the Netherlands East Indies as 'ownerless property' which would be seized by Britain and America unless it were 'secured for Asia'. He urged that Japan should at least demand preferential rights there. In his speech celebrating the Tripartite Alliance, he warned that this would become a dead letter if not actively turned to account. With his taste for historical parallels, he likened the intellectuals who were now debating the implications of the alliance to the ill-fated sixteenth century figure Akechi Mitsuhide, who, after destroying Nobunaga, was so preoccupied with studying the theory of the shogunate that he allowed the man of action, Hideyoshi, to seize the commanding heights of Tennōzan and accomplish his ruin. Nakano urged Japan to seize 'our Tennōzan in the South', whose resources would enable Japan to attain self-reliance against all comers.[147]

With General Itagaki, he tended to discount the likelihood of United States intervention but claimed that even if this occurred it would be less effective at this stage than it might be later, in view of that country's present commitments in Europe. As already noted, he hoped that such a strategic breakthrough would solve the China problem and later stated an argument that may have been in his mind earlier—that Japanese control of Southeast Asian resources would make exploitation of China less necessary, while the prospect of China's sharing in them might well win China over to the co-prosperity conception.

The highest point in Nakano's campaign for the Southern Advance and, indeed, his whole career as a mass agitator, was reached on the First of May 1941, which had now been designated Asia Development and Public Duty Day. Proceedings began in the afternoon with a special national congress of the Tōhōkai, this being followed by a pilgrimage to the palace and the Yasukuni shrine for the war dead by 3000 members of the Youth Corps. The marchers were then used to control a huge mass meeting at the Ryōgoku wrestling amphitheatre, attended by well over 100 000 people.

Here, flanked by giant banners with slogans calling for a new structure of 'political participation by the whole people', 'Asia for the Asians' and the seizure of the NEI, Nakano spoke for four hours urging an immediate advance before Britain and the United States established an impregnable fortified arc through the South Seas. The recently concluded Neutrality Pact with the Soviet Union had freed Japan for such a venture but a new obstacle was now being presented by the negotiations with the United States initiated by the government in a last bid for a solution to the China problem short of war. As Nakano described these talks:

> To control an onrushing bull, you have to get it by the snout. That is, you control it by its weakest point. Now that our country is aroused to make the Southern Advance, the Anglo–American trick is to hold us back through our weakest spot—the upper classes.[148]

But he discounted any real American willingness to fight.

Evidence of continued hostility by the traditionalist right appears in a reference of this speech to the obstruction of Tōhōkai meetings by 'professional rightists and hired gangsters'. But there are various signs that Nakano was attempting to conciliate the National Polity party. One is a much increased emphasis on the Emperor myth and Restorationist rhetoric—which was also a reasonable precaution against official suppression on ideological grounds. There are two censorship deletions in the published version of this speech, one relating to the status of political associations and one to the 'opium of flattery of Britain and America'. Regarding the Emperor's role, he says:

> What solicitude His Majesty must feel over these ever-shifting and changing cabinets and this unsettled national policy!... His Majesty cannot resign. His responsibility is absolute and infinite... With cabinets of this kind, more particularly as time and circumstances demand, we must utterly ignore them and demonstrate our loyalty directly to those around His Majesty who, with absolute responsibility, is making untiring efforts for the homeland.[149]

Nakano now repeatedly defines his agitation as aimed at influencing the Emperor's immediate advisers—which may be seen as a further retreat, enforced by circumstances, from the rational political processes preferred by him during the more effective parts of his career. He also now made less use of the term 'totalism', preferring others such as 'national community' (*kokumin kyōdōtai*) or 'great family state' which could be used in arguments of the same kind but were more consistent with the National Polity conception of total national solidarity without party or other sectional loyalties.

Another mode of approach to the traditionalist right was his occasional appearance on behalf of the defence in trials for terrorism of figures associated with it. He had already done this in the trial of the 1933 'Divine Warrior' (*Shimpeitai*) conspirators begun in 1939, and in April 1941 he welcomed the acquittal of the accused. In June he testified for the defence of Homma Kenichirō of Mito, formerly Tōyama's personal aide, who was being tried for plotting to assassinate the former Lord Privy Seal Yuasa. In court Nakano attacked the 'status quo forces' as consisting of '200 upper class families' who rotated cabinet formation among themselves.[150]

After the May First rally the Tōhōkai held a campaign to collect 1 000 000 signatures petitioning for the Southern Advance, but the situation took an unfavourable turn when Germany invaded the Soviet Union and the Japanese government began to lean towards the alternative of moving against the latter while making serious efforts for a settlement with the United States. Soon afterwards, Nakano went on a speaking tour to Hokkaido, accompanied by his son Yasuo, and although his meetings were well attended he experienced a greater degree of police suppression than usual. His last meeting was dissolved by police order—apparently a new experience. An address 'In Reply to Roosevelt and Churchill', in which he attacked the Atlantic Charter as a perpetuation of 'world feudalism', was so severely censored on being issued as a pamphlet that its length was cut by 107 lines.

Under these conditions, the emergence of the Tōjō cabinet seemed a favourable turn of events and a Tōhōkai statement welcomed Tōjō's joint holding of the seats of prime minister and war and home ministers, as a sign of greater readiness for strong action.[151] Nakano held a rally calling for decisive measures (though not fully specified) and when the war began at Pearl Harbour he hailed it with a statement that the Tōhōkai had 'demonstrated the loyalty of the masses and been the outrider in facing the crisis'.

He telephoned Ogata to ask whether he had any inside information but none was to hand because of the *Asahi*'s poor relations with the army. Ogata speaks of his tone of voice as being full of doubt and from this argues that Nakano had not wished the Southern Advance to take the form of a direct attack on the United States. Nakano Yasuo, however, with his usual greater frankness, suggests that his father's real purpose was to have Ogata help him decide what to do about a rally previously set for 17 December.

This rally finally took the form of a celebration of the war's initial successes, the Asian peoples to be liberated being represented by Indian and Indonesian guests, as well as an aged Turk named Ibrahim. Here Nakano called for a complete end to any internal divisiveness in view of the trials to come, quoting Saigō's conciliation of the defeated Shōnai clan as an example.[152]

But he permitted himself some expression of uneasiness at the Emergency Law for the Control of Speech, Publication, Assembly and Association just then being passed through the Diet, which his Diet following led by Mitamura were vainly trying to block. Here again, however, he could only protest in terms of the Emperor myth and particularly referred to Emperor Meiji's approach to the great emergencies of his time. His Charter Oath had provided the model for meeting crises by relying on his subjects' initiative—his confidence in his people being such that his only fear was that they might not be active enough, rather than that there was any need to restrain them.

For the time being, the overwhelming success of Japanese arms left Nakano without any basis for criticism or room for a distinctive policy. He spoke about this to his son Yasuo, who though not well versed in the situation reassured him that Tōjō was bound to make some mistakes, so his father should always be ready to resume a critical posture. Mitamura alleges that after the fall of Singapore Nakano began an undercover campaign to have peace negotiations opened from the position of maximum military advantage. Moves of this sort are mentioned elsewhere too, but Nakano's commitment to them is doubtful in view of his arguments in the succeeding election campaign condemning premature peace moves, since owing to the enemy's greater long-term resources a peace short of decisive victory would be a mere truce.[153]

Before long Nakano, along with much of the civilian right, felt impelled to take a stand against Tōjō over his plans for the Diet election due in April 1942. These moves may be seen as a renewal of the army mainstream's earlier abortive hopes of making the IRAA into a single national political entity. But now, instead of giving the 'Restorationist camp' the prominence it had enjoyed in Konoe's Preparatory Committee, Tōjō chose as his instrument a group of 33 'representatives of all fields', consisting largely of financiers and party men like Nagai. Suetsugu and Tokutomi represented ultranationalist opinion but, far from being in any way Restorationist or 'renovationist', these were now well adjusted to the prevailing power structure. The 33 under General Abe, formed a Council for an Imperial Rule Assistance Election to recommend the return of candidates who would be amenable to the government's purposes. This system of candidature by quasi-official recommendation through a body of prominent citizens had already been tried out in some local elections and was defended on the grounds that it was better to base electoral procedures on candidates' being called upon to stand rather than leave it to their personal initiative.

Although the option remained of seeking recommendation, as was done sucessfully by a number of Japanist groups, and by Hashimoto, the Tōhōkai and most of the traditionalist right opposed the arrangement. Nakano attacked the authorities for not recognising those elements who had rallied the nation against the pro-Anglo American conservatives but were now being put aside in favour of a comeback by the old-liners—a process which he described by the proverb: 'When the hare is killed the hound is cooked.'[154] Akao Bin also complained of the absence on the Council of representatives of the renovationist camp or Japanist camp and successfully contested the election without recommendation, along with several kindred figures. Other dissenting candidates were of former party background, notably in Hatoyama's Dōkōkai.

The Tōhōkai was the biggest opposition group contesting the election, fielding 47 candidates. Nakano's campaign centred on the two main issues of East Asian relations and the controlled economy, now in an advanced stage of implementation. On the first, he showed some insight into issues which were to prove crucial. He warned, for example, against an attitude of superiority to other East Asian races, pointing out that while the Annamese had accepted French tyranny through a sense of helplessness, they would be more resentful of a Japanese tyranny, through feeling a right to be regarded as equals by fellow Asians. He also stressed that although the resources of Southeast Asia would be paid for in military currency, Japan would have to maintain an adequate supply of essential commodities available for purchase with such currency so that it would not become valueless—even at great cost to Japanese standards of consumption.[155] These were the aspects in which Japan failed most fatally in the occupied areas, though in regard to economic policy there were of course strict limits to what Japan could achieve in the supply of commodities given the level of industrial development at the time.

Nakano's approach to economic policy was based on his submission to the IRAA Board of Directors regarding the Kikakuin Plan. The warning example he used was the situation in Germany during the First World War, when the national effort and morale were allegedly undermined by the dominance of Jewish 'privileged capital' in league with an unenlightened bureaucracy. Japan was now exposed to the imminent danger of a similar vicious combination of 'bureaucratic expediency' and monopolistic profiteering. The Tōhōkai's task was to ensure that the masses' conditions were made known.

Nakano and six other Tōhōkai candidates were elected, perhaps a creditable performance under the prevailing conditions of severe official harassment, indicated by the limited proportion of unrecommended candidates who were elected—85 out of 466 seats. The result was, however, seen by Nakano as a serious defeat, as his aim had been to gain at least 20 seats.[156]

After the election, the successful recommended candidates were incorporated into a party called the Imperial Rule Assistance Political Society (*Yokusan Seijikai*) and the government indicated that it would no longer recognise any other political association. Ogata and Tokutomi therefore used their influence to obtain approval for the Tōhōkai Diet members' affiliation to the IRAPS, while the party was converted into a non-political association for moral thought (*shisō kessha*) under the name of Tōhō Dōshikai (Orient Comrades Society). This retained the auxiliary organs established under the Shintōsha, with a society periodical called the *Tōhō Jihō* (Orient Review).

Protests at the Tōhōkai's dissolution flooded in from all over the country, and in view of the danger that some members might turn to violence Nakano wrote an elaborate justification along the lines that the Tōhōkai had after all originally been a cultural body operating on a plane above that of day-to-day politics, in the sense of the functioning of established institutions on which no divisions were any longer permissible. The party was just returning to this role and its spirit was indestructible. He added, however, that he 'felt as if the fatigue of twelve years' bitter struggle had come upon him all at once'.[157]

The Tōhō Dōshikai (apart from the Youth Corps) initially had branches in twenty prefectures as well as Tokyo, with about 14 490 members.[158] Its level of activity declined rapidly, however, and Nakano is said to have now begun to entertain doubts about his career. He wondered whether he might not have done better to keep to writing or scholarship, especially when old friends commented that his early journalistic work (for example, the *Meiji Minken Shiron*) was far more valuable than anything he had written as a politician.

He now had leisure to return to more scholarly pursuits and for a time was chiefly occupied in lecturing for his Shintōjuku Academy on a variety of Chinese and Japanese classics, but especially on the late Tokugawa loyalist historian Rai Sanyō. Two major series of lectures dealt with Hideyoshi and the short-lived but celebrated Kemmu Restoration of 1333. The former, treating Hideyoshi as a 'true representative of the Japanese race' of plebeian stock, was published in 1943 and sold 75 000 copies; the latter was also published after the war.

Nakano now presented a parallel to his hero Saigō's withdrawal to his private school after losing political influence in 1873 and the parallel would later be strengthened by a last, ill-fated bid for power.

5
A final stand for survival with honour

The island of Kyushu is noted for several highly active volcanoes which rarely fall dormant and, if this should chance to occur, can reliably be predicted to erupt again before long with renewed fury. There seems to be a tradition that the 'sons of Kyushu' share this feature of their natural background, as seen in the well-known verse, sometimes quoted by Nakano, where the early Fukuoka loyalist Hirano Kuniomi compares the fulminations of Sakurajima with his own restless ardour:

> When set beside the passions that flame within my heart, Your smoking is but faint, Mount Sakurajima!

It might similarly have been predicted of Nakano, especially in view of his past record, that even during the middle months of 1942, when he was more subdued than for any comparable period of his career, the pressures making for new eruptions were simmering not far below the surface. Meanwhile he had to resort to vicarious outlets for his pent-up energies by contemplating and discussing the heroic episodes of past eras, at the same time hoping that seeds planted in his listeners' minds would prepare them for new efforts when the occasion arose. His lectures on the Kemmu Restoration were well enough executed to be thought worth publishing ten years later—though, as he wrote at the time, he was not lecturing as a specialist but for the purpose of commenting on current events and his own experiences.

As he was—for reasons which will become apparent—under increasingly close surveillance by Special Higher ('Thought') Police and *Kempeitai* (military police), he had little alternative to speaking in the terms of National Polity or Restorationist rhetoric, though he had an added motive for this in that he was cultivating the Japanist front who were steadily growing more hostile to the Tōjō regime. In conveying more distinctive viewpoints of his own, he was obliged to resort to more or less oblique historical allusions, often displaying much of his usual ironic wit.

For example, he deplored the fact that, despite Kusunoki Masahige's great military genius, his modest status of Lower Fifth court rank ('one step lower than Nakano's own') prevented direct access to the Emperor (as he himself had to contemplate manoeuvres through the Senior Statesmen). The Emperor Go-Daigo was not lacking in ability but had not experienced enough hardship and was out of touch with the people's conditions (his usual description of Prince Konoe). The first use of paper money under Go-Daigo, leading to inflation, extravagance and the attempted curbing of this by a mass of regulations including the standardisation of costumes (like the current national uniform which Nakano often derided) had obvious parallels. The honest courtier Fujiwara Fujifusa took the opportunity to admonish the Emperor when he was admiring a prize horse because the court was so crowded with sycophants that he had little chance to approach him.

> Sycophants really seem to do well around the great, don't they? When someone becomes a factory manager, a party leader, or still more so a prime minister [!], if he is not extremely resolute, petty characters will get at his weaknesses and tender spots.[159]

Nakano quotes the sycophant courtiers' assertion that, whatever happens, Heaven will sustain the loyalist forces, as a clear enough allusion to current official propaganda on the invincibility of the 'divine' Imperial Army. By way of conciliating the National Polity camp, however, he speaks of the native Japanese doctrine of 'direct imperial rule' (*shinseiron*) as a necessary corrective for foreign models (doubtless including nazism to which he now seldom referred except in a perfunctory way in *Tōtairiku* news commentaries). But he qualifies the more extreme interpretations of this principle by arguing that no matter how divine (*arahitogami*) he may be, the Emperor could not manage every detail of government personally, so that direct rule really means joint government by the whole 'familial state' as against usurpation by particular privileged elements.

Later in 1942 Nakano erupted into a series of political moves which were prompted partly by widespread dissatisfaction with the newly established economic control associations and partly by growing concern at the military situation after the naval defeat at Midway and the first setbacks in the Solomons. He was obtaining privileged information on the war from army monitors of Allied broadcasts[160]—

an indication of continued contacts with non-Tōjō factions in the army—and now admitted that it was no easy task to exploit the potential resources of the occupied areas.[161]

Nakano's first public appearance in Tokyo for some time was at a Symposium on the Prosecution of a Long-term War, where he appeared with the top bureaucratic planner, Kishi Nobusuke, minister for commerce and industry, as well as another official. Here he was incensed by Kishi's call for higher morale to combat the 'Anglo–America within' or the 'Jewish mentality' of elements in the economy which were not submitting fully to the economic control structure.

Soon afterwards, Nakano elaborated his counter-argument and its whole supporting philosophy in two major speeches that launched him on a collision course with the Tōjō regime. The first, delivered at Waseda under the title 'The World prospers through the Individual' (*Tenka ichinin o motte okoru*), is often referred to as his greatest speech. It is certainly of unusual interest, doubtless having benefited from a sophisticated audience and from his recent reading and reflections. It is also described as marking a return to his earlier liberalism after his fascist interlude, but does not show any basic discontinuity, as Nakano had consistently attacked the new bureaucrats, while he also still continued to quote Hitler. It might best be described as his last political testament, as he had no opportunity to develop his thought further.

The title comes from a classical Chinese saying: 'A state prospers through the individual and is ruined through the individual'. Beginning with a survey of the difficult military position, Nakano enlarged on the irony of a situation where officials responsible for material production, such as Kishi, placed their central emphasis on issues of morale. Making prominent use of Yōmeigaku terminology, he pointed out that a grasp of principles (*ri*) was meaningless without the drive (*ki*) to implement them. He illustrated this point with Saigō's saying that 'extremists are the nation's treasure'—a rebuke to merely theorising intellectuals.

He further censured Kishi's distinction between the 'Anglo–American' or 'Jewish' profit motive, associated with liberalism, and the 'Japanese spirit' of utterly selfless service, pointing out that long before Western influence was felt, Mitsui, Kōnoike and the proverbial Zeniya Gohei had assiduously sought profit. Nor need this be condemned, so long as private initiative and creativity were guided by the public interest, in contrast with the stifling of their organic life by the mechanical conformity of bureaucratic controlism. The latter, as he had often argued before, was the real 'Jewish mentality'.

Nakano reviewed historically the growth of bureaucratic control in

Japan. Before the Manchurian Incident, he said, the futile alternation of 'positive' and 'negative' policies was attacked both by right-wing opponents of liberalism and pacifism, and by left-wing intellectuals. Of the latter, many suffered suppression but the less committed entered the bureaucracy and comfortably grew out of their radicalism. When reform became essential after Manchuria, the army, as its primary advocate, rejected the parties but had to replace them in their political role with the new bureaucrats, whose only theoretical resource was the semi-leftist residue from their student days. So they adopted an unreasoning policy of rationalisation by amalgamation, putting quantity before quality and combining the evils of monopoly capitalism and state control. Nakano cited concrete cases, uncovered by his Youth Corps' investigations.

Returning to basic theory, he condemned the current fashion of disparaging all liberalism as Anglo–American ideology. Praising the slogan: 'Give me liberty or give me death!', he interpreted it as affirming the ultimate responsibility of the individual, which can achieve more than any system of compulsion. Itagaki Taisuke's pioneer liberalism, he said, was wholly Japanese and patriotic in that it had arisen from his observing how, during the campaign to crush opposition to the Restoration, the peasantry in the hostile fief of Aizu were utterly indifferent to the outcome because feudalism had deprived them of all sense of public involvement and responsibility. Itagaki had therefore aimed to provide the Japanese people with the social stake and commitment to ensure their every effort for their country's greatness. Japanese liberalism was thus not anti-monarchical, as its Western counterpart often was, but only opposed to an officialdom denying the people's rights. Saigō's standpoint was similar.

Inverting Kishi's approach, Nakano went on to advocate a policy of incentives for the masses and sacrifice from those in positions of leadership, as the latter should be those most endowed with public spirit (as patriots). He waxed particularly emotional over the example of Clemenceau, who at the time of France's greatest peril had swept aside the corrupt administration, won over the rebellious workers and inspired the troops by personal exhortation at the front. It was clear enough that Nakano hoped for another Clemenceau to arise in Japan to save the current situation—a role which he would be more than ready to play himself, though in Japanese style it might be necessary to have a more senior figure as the title lead.

After exhorting the students each to write his own *Mein Kampf* in his life, Nakano closed with a call to abandon opportunism, the root of all evils:

The great ship of Japan is adrift in heavy seas—in danger from a full complement of opportunists. Awaken for yourselves! Let the world prosper through the individual! This is my earnest hope of my beloved fellow alumni.[162]

He repeated this speech in more popularised form at Hibiya Hall under the title 'Form a national battle-line for certain victory!'— though here he added a discouragement to 'direct action' (terrorism) as being a case of mere drive (*ki*) without guiding principles (*ri*).[163] The police did not interfere, probably owing to the enthusiasm of the large crowd—4000 having paid the usual 30 *sen* to fill the hall to capacity while twice the number gathered outside.

After this, however, the authorities lost no time in banning any further public speaking by Nakano or any Tōhō Dōshikai members. Banning and censorship of *Tōtairiku* were intensified and even the New Year's Day 1943 issue of the *Asahi* was banned for carrying an article by Nakano on wartime prime ministers. Although this spoke through guarded historical allusions some of these were rather telling, for example the point that Generals Hindenburg and Ludendorff were great in the field, but when placed in supreme control of the war failed to put a proper trust in the people, instead restricting them and 'trampling on their patriotism by imposing a servile drudgery'.[164]

With such curbs on public expression, protest against the Tōjō regime's policies concentrated in the Diet, where it was pressed by an incongruous alliance of rightists and former party liberals. The new right wing Dietmen (whether originally recommended or not) had so far contributed little, through inexperience in this arena. Some of them, however, alongside the Tōhō Dōshikai, now took the lead in opposing the use of the recommendation system in the prefectural elections due in 1943 and Tōjō assured them that the system would not be officially sanctioned.

The next round of protests was directed against the amended Special Law for Wartime Crimes which was introduced in March to outlaw any move aimed at the disturbance of the National government. Opposition in the usual deliberative committee was led by Nakano's lieutenant Mitamura, probably because of his legal background as a colonial ministry police officer. He argued that to prohibit any initiative towards changing a particular cabinet would transform it into a dictatorship unchallengeable by constitutional process.

Extra-Diet patriotic societies lobbied and agitated intensively against the proposed law. Since such moves to strengthen the government were associated with plans for tighter economic controls, so threatening the Zaibatsu's considerable share in the control system, it is likely enough that the alliance between Zaibatsu and Japanists against the early IRAA was still continuing. At the same time, some part must have been played by emotional factors, such as resentment for the extreme right's meagre share of influence—though this again might be increased by pressure on the government. An alliance of fifteen right-wing groups, including the Tōhō Dōshikai, between them distributed several pamphlets, condemning the Bill as giving the government of the day an inviolability equal to the eternal National Polity and thus amounting to a new shogunate. A prominent extra-Diet spokesman was Amano Tatsuo, a lawyer of singular fanaticism who had been active in the Shimpeitai conspiracy and was now in the Kinnō Makoto-musubi (Loyalist Band of Devotion). He wrote in the March 1943 *Ishin Kōron* that Tōjō was using the war to usurp the Emperor's prerogatives—like the Abbot Dōkyō in the Nara period, the Shoguns and other such villains of the Restorationist creed—and described him as 'a traitor and rebel destroying the tranquil order of the National Polity' who was dominated by 'pseudo-recanters' from communism.[165] As a result he was arrested for a time. These right-wing efforts were supported in the Diet by party liberals like Hatoyama and Miki Bukichi, but the grip of the IRAPS on most Diet members saw the Bill through.

A similar confrontation occurred in a special Diet session called in June 1943 to pass two important economic control measures, when the right wing, including the Tōhō Dōshikai, formed a 'Pearl Harbour Day Society' to coordinate opposition. But as the three-day session would be restricted to formalities, the only chance to protest was at an IRAPS members' meeting, where Hatoyama, Miki and Nakano took a vigorous joint stand and Nakano denounced the corruption of government by 'sycophants' (*chabōzudomo*). Upon Akao Bin's expulsion from the IRAPS for rebuking Tōjō in the House, Nakano, Hatoyama and others resigned from the party.

The last round

Nakano was now urged by Miki to follow the course he himself was adopting—to retire from political activity as futile and hold himself in reserve against the possibility that, even in the extreme case of Japan's defeat, he might yet be capable of some future role. This hope was fully realised in his own case but Nakano could not accept such advice. He was not only temperamentally incapable of resigning himself to inactivity but also still harboured the wish to disprove the habitual gibe from the 'activist right' that he was 'good at making speeches but without capacity for effective action'. More importantly, however, as the gravity of Japan's external and internal situation became more clearly apparent, he was haunted by a growing sense of his share of responsibility for this disastrous course of events by his advocacy of such policies as the Tripartite Alliance, economic controls and the Southern Advance.

His subsequent activities are described by his then secretary Shintō as impelled not so much by explicit hopes as by a mood of desperation[166] and his utterances increasingly assume a reckless or even suicidal quality—suggesting a gamble for all or nothing. An article referring to Axis reverses in Europe speaks of the need to 'open a way to life in the midst of death'—the theme of a Zen conundrum, while a rather clear foreshadowing of Nakano's ultimate fate can be read in passages of his lectures on the Kemmu Restoration. Speaking of the death against hopeless odds of its great tragic hero, Masashige, he says: 'If he had not died in this battle, he would not be Masashige. It is in his death that Masashige is revealed ... It is not so moving merely to read about him. It is moving to read while reflecting on oneself'. Of another fallen hero he says: 'A man must decide his mission and carry it through ... But if it is impossible to continue living, it is because one's own efforts or abilities have fallen short. Heaven is not to be resented, or man blamed'.

Being cornered in both Diet and public forums, Nakano's last resort was to take part in covert moves to oust Tōjō which had been developing for some time in certain sections of the Establishment. These elements were growing perturbed at the signs of strategic weakness and at Tōjō's failure to define his war aims in terms which might enable some tolerable settlement to be reached. Nakano could offer to contribute something in the way of popular backing, as the high sales of his *Hideyoshi* demonstrated that he and his ideas still commanded widespread favour.

Details of the anti-Tōjō movement are naturally difficult to establish fully, because considerations of secrecy prevented the survival of much contemporary evidence, while postwar accounts are naturally suspect. One early development was a reported meeting at the home of Yoshida Shigeru of the Foreign Office, including Kojima Kazuo, Ikeda of Mitsui and military men of the Imperial Way faction, who canvassed the possibility of a cabinet headed by General Ugaki, apparently the most widely acceptable army figure. Prince Konoe was obsessed with the danger of communist subversion if the war were prolonged or ended too disastrously, while Hiranuma, furthest to the right of the former premiers, suspected Tōjō himself of 'red ideas'.

Within the administration, Matsumae Shigeyoshi of the communications ministry collated a 150 page report on the technical weaknesses of war production and circulated it to the former premiers and to navy circles, including Prince Takamatsu, a captain and the Emperor's brother. A senior research officer in the Planning

Board, Tanabe Tadao, wrote an article in the January *Chūō Kōron* with a critical note that caught Nakano's attention. At another level, a plot by right wing students of the Takushoku University to assassinate Tōjō was uncovered in June.

The only realistic possibility for the anti-Tōjō movement to succeed was to mobilise the Senior Statesmen, who had acquired the function of nominating prime ministers, a group consisting of all former premiers, the Lord Privy Seal Kido Kōichi and the president of the Privy Council. The weak link here was Kido, who had been largely responsible for Tōjō's appointment and was unwilling to contemplate a change of cabinet in wartime, so did his best to inform Tōjō of any moves against him and kept the Emperor largely isolated from other elements. The Emperor is also described at this time as being afraid of Imperial Way influence as likely to threaten relations with the Soviet Union, because of that faction's near-paranoid preoccupation with the communist threat.

Nakano did not regard the Senior Statesmen as promising material and spoke of them as needing constant winding up like marionettes. He had attacked all of them with some degree of bitterness in the past, sometimes—ironically now—for being lukewarm about warlike policies, but he realised that there was no other possible avenue of action. So he built up a network of collaborators in an effort to work on them.

He formed a particularly close alliance with Amano, whose anti-Tōjō article in the *Ishin Kōron* had impressed him, though Amano's earlier association with terrorism would be a liability from the viewpoint of the Senior Statesmen. Contact was made with Matsumae by visiting him in hospital and with Tanabe through one of the ubiquitous natives of Fukuoka, called Hinoshita, who was on his staff. Nakano arranged for Tanabe to visit Konoe and, subsequently, with Hinoshita's help, to compile a 'Plan for the Reconstruction of the War Economy'.

Further data on the private sector of the economy were obtained through Tsuda Shingo of Kanebō, who maintained steady support for Nakano during this period. Nakano also maintained links with the General Staff, even receiving funds from that quarter, as this is described as the source of ¥5000 which he entrusted to his son on his arrest.

Immediately after leaving the IRAPS, Nakano visited Higashikuni, an Imperial Prince and member of the Supreme War Council, with whom he had earlier been in contact and who had already sometimes been considered as a potential prime minister—the role that finally fell to him at the war's end. His diary notes Nakano's sense of his own and the Diet's share of responsibility for the situation. This contact seems to have worried Tōjō's party most and their next move toward Nakano at this stage was conciliatory—an offer to appoint him president of the Information Bureau, for which his journalistic background well qualified him. He naturally refused to serve a regime in whose fall he saw Japan's only hope.[167]

The frankest account of Nakano's aims is given by his youth leader Nagata Masayoshi who relates that, since he recognised that violence could only provoke martial law, he hoped by political means to realise a new structure whereby the irrational domination of the military and the control bureaucrats would be set aside and essential functions entrusted to those best qualified in each field. Strategically, the war of attrition on the mainland would be reduced to a minimum and the army and navy air arms unified, in order to concentrate the greatest war potential against the United States for a decisive battle which would convince the Allies of the need for a settlement short of unconditional surrender.[168]

Nakano even made an attempt to influence the Emperor himself on the occasion of an audience granted a Fukuoka contact, the head of the Coal Control Association, but Kido's vigilance prevented his report from leading to any serious questioning of government policy. Nakano's moves culminated in a plan to convince the Senior Statesmen of Tōjō's unfitness for office and to have them induce him to relinquish the premiership so as to concentrate on military operations as chief of the General Staff. He would be replaced by General Ugaki, whom Nakano now described to his son as a 'Clemenceau'—a military man being essential at this stage to purge the army. The Imperial Way faction's General Yanagawa is quoted as estimating that a purge of about ten Tōjō faction leaders from headquarters staff would do.[169]

Nakano's closest financial backer, Yasukawa, recalls Nakano consulting him about a suitable candidate to combine the functions of minister for commerce and industry and president of the Planning Board—jurisdictional clashes between these being notorious. Nakano mentioned that he himself would be home minister, Hirota foreign minister and Ogata president of the Information Bureau.[170] Other candidates mentioned elsewhere were the Imperial Way faction's General Obata Toshishirō as war minister, Admiral Toyoda Soemu as navy minister, Hatoyama as minister for agriculture and Amano as cabinet secretary.

The campaign was coordinated on a visit at the end of July to the mountain resort of Karuizawa where Konoe, Ugaki and Hatoyama had their villas. As well as taking his son, Nakano was accompanied by Amano and his son, Mitamura and Hinoshita. Matsumae travelled separately and called on Konoe, asking him to work on the Emperor, while Hinoshita took his and Tanabe's 'reconstruction plan' to all three prominent figures. Nakano Yasuo recalls delivering a sealed message to Konoe's villa and making a telephone appointment with Ugaki at one of several dinners to which Hatoyama treated the conspirators. Despite recurrent signs of police surveillance of their moves, Nakano returned to Tokyo in an optimistic mood. Yoshida Shigeru happened to be travelling on the same train.

Soon afterwards, Mitamura prepared a pamphlet under his own name entitled 'The Management of the IRAPS and the *Kokutai* Constitution', explaining the reasons for his leaving the IRAPS. In it, he attacked the single national party system as a new shogunate and denounced the manner in which Tōjō's monolithic regime fusing government, IRAPS and IRAA deprived the Diet of its constitutional function of surveillance of the executive. 'It is essential to leave open an avenue for criticising the administration. Without criticism there is no reflection. Without reflection there is no improvement. Criticism provides the drive for dedicated effort and such effort is the nation's treasure.'[171] Two thousand copies were distributed by the Tōhō Dōshikai to Diet members, ministers, Privy Councillors, newspapers and prominent intellectuals, though a ban on its publication naturally soon followed.

Concrete moves by the Senior Statesmen began when Okada's son-in-law, in a meeting with Kido, suggested that Tōjō might be appointed chief of the General Staff and step down as prime minister. Kido replied that this might be done if demanded by 'public opinion' which, on being pressed, he added might be regarded as represented by a consensus of the Senior Statesmen. Okada therefore obtained the agreement of the ex-premiers to meet Tōjō at the Peers' Club on 30 August 1943, inviting him to come alone in the hope that they could speak frankly and pursue Tōjō's personal responsibility for the government's performance. With Kido's encouragement, however, Tōjō insisted on being accompanied by his usual Liaison Conference aides (foreign, finance and navy ministers and president of the Planning Board), with the result that the Senior Statesmen were unable to exert the necessary pressure. Okada in any case thought that haste might spoil matters and was content for the moment to establish the habit of such encounters with Tōjō,[172] which played its part in Tōjō's ultimate fall from power.

Nakano meanwhile gave an address to the Tōhō Dōshikai on the need to restore the army to its proper role and on 30 August, with Amano and Mitamura, he waited at the Society's headquarters for word from Konoe. When none was received they telephoned the Peers' Club, only to be told that the meeting had long dispersed and that Konoe had returned direct to Karuizawa.

Though bitterly disappointed, Nakano recovered his spirit to some degree on confirming that the Senior Statesmen had not abandoned their ultimate aim. But Tōjō's counterattack began a few days later with Mitamura's arrest. He was initially questioned for a week by censorship officials about his pamphlet, then at greater length by the Special Higher Police on suspicion of infringing the Special Law for Wartime Crimes, as well as an actual case of incitement of right-wing students to assassinate Tōjō by a member of Amano's Makoto-musubi group. A copy of the prospective Ugaki cabinet seems to have come into police possession. He stood up well under questioning, however, sustained by his legal and practical experience as a former colonial ministry police officer.

Tōjō's counterattack moved into higher gear with an Imperial Conference on 30 September which attempted to strike a balance between Japan's needs and capabilities for replacing the existing level of aircraft and shipping losses. The Greater East Asia Conference was also fixed for November, to be attended by Japan's client governments in the co-prosperity sphere. During this Imperial Conference the president of the Privy Council expressed concern about reports of army-navy disharmony but was assured that they were groundless. A Diet session was then fixed for 26 October to implement the government's own solution to the war economy's ills by a unified War Procurement Ministry under Kishi and it was then decided to arrest Nakano to prevent him using this opportunity to develop an anti-Tōjō movement in the Diet.

It had been hoped to arrest him earlier on some substantial charge but the head of the Thought Section of the Procurator-General's Office, Nakamura Toneo, refused to authorise this, as Mitamura's examination had failed to produce adequate evidence. The procurators seem to have been unfavourably disposed to Tōjō, feeling it to be their duty, as officials of the justice ministry, to restrain police and *Kempeitai* excesses. Besides, in view of Hiranuma's influence in that ministry, they may well have also regarded Tōjō with mistrust as a threat to the National Polity.

Nakano's last public appearance was at a court case where he spoke in defence of Makoto-musubi members who had severely injured Hiranuma in mid-1941 in retaliation for his ousting Matsuoka Yōsuke from the cabinet. Early on 21 October he was provisionally arrested on police initiative, along with all office-holders of the Tōhō Dōshikai, the Makoto-musubi and the Fukuoka Kinnō Dōshikai— over 100 in all. He managed to pass his son a copy of the 'Reconstruction of the War Economy' to dispose of, as well as ¥80 000 (including ¥5000 in General Staff funds) to entrust to Ogata, before the police seized all other documents, together with eleven swords.

As all police records on this case were destroyed in subsequent bombing, the basic authority on events during Nakano's custody is Ogata, who as president of the Information Bureau under the next cabinet was in a good position to investigate the circumstances of his friend's death. His account is also generally confirmed by Procurator-General Matsusaka Hiromasa, who was directly involved.[173] Inomata, using data collected by the Seigō Society, also quotes at least 25 miscellaneous sources (largely magazine articles) bearing on Nakano's death, which vary widely in detail.

Although the police attempted to obtain from Nakano a confession to spreading false rumours little progress was made, as their spies were already well informed about his activities without being able to formulate enough evidence to satisfy the procurators. Meanwhile Hatoyama and others agitated in the Diet offices against the improper detention of two Diet members without charge.

At a meeting called at Tōjō's residence on 24 October to force a quick decision, Procurator-General Matsusaka denied that grounds existed to charge Nakano, while the dominant figure in the IRAPS, Ōasa Tadao, warned that the Diet would not accept Nakano's confinement without charge during a session, contrary to Article 53 of the Constitution. Faced with such resistance by both the Judiciary and the Legislature, Tōjō fell back on his immediate power base, the *Kempeitai*—his close henchman, Colonel Shikata Ryōji, then undertaking to obtain a confession from Nakano in time for a charge to be laid next day to prevent his attendance at the Diet on 26 October.

Early in the morning Nakano was secretly removed from his cell and at noon the *Kempeitai* informed the Procurator-General's Office of his confession to spreading rumours that disharmony between the army and the navy had led to the loss of Guadalcanal. Ogata's first thought on later hearing of the confession was the possibility of torture, but there was no sign of this on Nakano's body a couple of days later.

One of Nakano's brief suicide notes gives a clue to the understandably obscure circumstances of his confession. It runs: 'A moment's decision, words flowed without hesitation, hoping to gain three days' respite, a nonsensical confession, no blame for anyone'. This is thought to indicate that he expected, in exchange for the confession, to be allowed to return home and perhaps attend the Diet session, though his release happened for other reasons.

Procurator Nakamura now had no choice but to take a statement from Nakano in order to apply to the District Court for a formal charge, which he still hoped not to be serious enough to warrant Nakano's continued detention. He ignored a fatuous supplementary charge of *lèse majesté* suggested by the *Kempeitai* on the basis of contacts with Prince Higashikuni.

When Nakano arrived, however, Nakamura was struck by his air of 'Oriental resignation', which suggested in retrospect that he had already decided on suicide. The phrase 'no blame for anyone' could indicate that he hoped his own removal from the scene might at least spare others from involvement. It was also later recalled that he had once spoken of death as preferable to imprisonment for one of his restless nature, particularly with a physical handicap.

It was 9 pm when the application reached the examining judge then on duty, Kobayashi Kenji, who had been led to expect a charge of *lèse majesté*. But on learning that the charge was the much lesser one of false rumours, he ruled that since, according to Itō's commentary on the Constitution, the Diet session was regarded as beginning on the day of convocation preceding the actual sitting, Nakano could not be held without either a charge being laid or the Diet's consent obtained before that date. The only charges allowing confinement during the session without Diet permission related to insurrection or foreign invasion.

On Nakano's being returned by the procurators to police headquarters, he was induced to sign an undertaking not to attend the Diet session and was lodged for the night in the duty room. Next morning, however, when about to return home, he was met by Shikata and detained for some hours at *Kempeitai* headquarters. What happened then is even more obscure than the details of their previous encounter. Shikata may well have urged upon Nakano the option of suicide as preferable to testing the *Kempeitai's* capacity for further persecution, so justifying his later reported boast that he had 'killed Nakano Seigō', among others.[174] A further clue is a remark made later to his son by a *kempei*: 'Your father was very worried about you both'. This seems to mean that, as Nakano's elder surviving son was already enlisted in the army and the younger about to be called up, Shikata could have threatened to victimise them, perhaps sending them to a war zone where there would be no hope of their survival. Evidence of this sort of measure by the Tōjō regime is afforded by the punitive call-ups of both Matsumae and Nakamura, among many others, in retaliation for their obstruction of Tōjō's purposes.

Nakano arrived home early in the afternoon, accompanied by a *kempei* who was later joined by another. He told his son, however: 'It's all over. I won't have to go there again'. The ambiguity of these phrases was realised only later, as also that of his message to Mitamura 'not to follow him'. In his mother's room he found a last remaining sword, which he removed 'to clean it'.

In the evening, after what turned out to be a farewell dinner with all family members within reach, he asked everyone to retire by ten o'clock in order to let him rest, while the two *kempei* were lodged in the guest room. Having earlier had the photographs of Hitler and Mussolini removed from his room, he replaced them with a statue of Masashige on horseback and one volume of a biography of Saigō. He was then occupied in writing farewell notes until, on the stroke of midnight, after making two cuts on his abdomen as a gesture to samurai tradition, he ended his life by cutting his carotid artery.

Upon the discovery of his body next morning, the two *kempei* escorts denied having noticed anything and suspicions directed towards them, which the local Higher Police were ready to follow up, were discounted by Nakano's personal physician. He also commented that this would not have happened if his wife had lived.

A number of brief notes were found in the family shrine, in an envelope addressed to Tōyama—which, Ishiwara later remarked, saved them from seizure by the police. They were directed to all Nakano's relatives, principal colleagues and various friends, even to his dead father, wife and sons, expressing the hope of reunion with them. Others cheered the imperial army, vowed to watch over the homeland (as Saigō had done), asked that the horses be properly cared for and expressed gratitude for the good fortune of a last gathering and the discovery of one remaining sword. Other notes by Nakano's body included a complaint of the sword's bluntness and his resignation from the Diet, suggesting the responsibility which he felt he shared with that institution for the dismal prospect now facing Japan.

Speculation about Nakano's motives for suicide and the surrounding circumstances was naturally rife, while the lore of *bushidō* associated with suicide was also a source of wide-ranging discussion. The two social groups most moved by the event were, on the one hand, the small businessman class which had provided the core of Nakano's following and, on the other, the ultranationalists whose ideology had been the source of so much of his rhetoric, especially in his earliest and latest phases. The first group were most in evidence at his funeral, which despite official discouragement was attended by 20 000 mourners, including a large cross-section from politics and journalism. One of Konoe's advisers, Itō Jusshi, is recorded as commenting:

> I was astonished at the grand scale of the funeral, rare in recent times ... There were twenty or thirty wreaths, flower-baskets and floral-arrangements, all from anonymous donors. When I enquired, I was told that they were mostly from individuals or bodies belonging to the humbler class of medium and smaller businessmen. In view of this, I would consider that it was not due to a simple feeling of devotion to Nakano, but that the indescribably tragic outlook that had pervaded this class of businessmen had been transformed into devotion to him.[175]

The traditionalist right seem to have been impressed. A couple of days later, at a Pan-Asianist rally in honour of Ras Bihari Bose, Tōyama was approached by a number of participants who admitted that they had misjudged Nakano in the past as a 'mere debater' and now wished to confess their error. Homma Kenichirō, a good representative of this group, describes Nakano's death as an 'atoning ablution' (*misogi*), going on to say:

> Our memorial offering to him is, as his rearguard, to carry on his struggle to banish the bureaucrats. What purpose would be served by the chanting of sutras by a thousand or a myriad monks? Even though we were to burn torches of incense and offer a forest of flowers, Nakano would not be satisfied. Blood can only be atoned for by blood.[176]

Nakano's epitaph was composed somewhat later by an ultranationalist of a different type—Tokutomi Sohō, who was protected by Tōjō's esteem from any untoward consequences. He includes an enigmatic judgement on Nakano's life and character, introducing a short summary of his career with the observation:

> Nakano Seigō took his life in his home at Shibuya, Tokyo, on the early morning of 27 October 1943. Nobody knows his reasons but, perceiving in his remains how unflinchingly he kept the rule of *bushidō*, one can only mark with grief that this did not happen by chance.[177]

Whatever Tokutomi precisely meant by this, Nakano's end was certainly in keeping with his character and career. It seems inevitable that he should prefer to die in the heat of a doomed struggle rather than live on into an existence of inaction and despair. Having played his last hand, he faced the negation of all he had ever striven for. So with his lifelong instinct for anticipating the trend of events, he became the forerunner of the hundreds of others who also could not bring themselves to survive Japan's defeat, but who left their final gesture until it had become a reality.

Reflections

The career of this turbulent yet resourceful man may best be placed in perspective by considering his relationship with the two social groups just referred to—small businessmen and 'professional' right wing activists. He is most usually treated as having developed into a leading example (or exemplar) of the latter group, who though diverse were distinguished in some degree by features which, as Najita puts it, 'could not be intrinsically related to the modern political framework'. But a closer examination suggests that he was throughout much more a characteristic member of the former class, though admittedly far more articulate and dynamic than usual for Japan.

His background, though nominally samurai, was much closer to the Hakata merchant community, his father's family having been engaged in water transport and then in pawnbroking, while his mother came of a sake brewing family and he himself was later long active in managing minor or regional journals. This background is sometimes given as an explanation for his ability at fundraising—which meant gaining the interest and support of hardheaded financiers, essentially by talking their kind of language. This of course is a feature that does clearly relate to the modern political process.

Most features of his political thought also set him apart from the 'activist right'. His opposition to any direct nationalisation of the economy distinguishes him from the state socialists; his advocacy of central planning runs counter to the stress on local autonomy by the Agrarianists; while unlike all elements in the right he avoided giving the imperial institution any central role in his political program, whether as an object of supreme devotion or as a lever for seizing power. He well realised that in practice it was a front for bureaucratic domination and at best hoped that it might be converted into a symbolic support for a populist movement opposing the monopoly of power by a privileged class—something more characteristic of bourgeois attitudes. As his son Tatsuhiko put it, he was no 'loyalist hero' (*kinnō shishi*). Nor was he much affected by the stress on Japanese uniqueness which accompanied the Emperor cult, being ready to borrow from European liberalism, Coles' rationalisation or fascist models without being inhibited by arguments that they were alien to the National Polity.

His Pan-Asianism, too, was not of the sentimental or 'adventurer' type but had two aspects more typical of bourgeois rationality—the positive aspect of economic expansion and the negative aspect of an outer line of defence against Anglo-American domination, one of his most consistent concerns. These two aspects produced his ambiguity on China, the former tending to coercion and the latter to conciliation—necessary to some extent if China were really to be an asset to Japan's defence.

Consistently with his basic drive to widen the political process so as to involve the nation as a whole, Nakano's most unvaried theme was his opposition to the influence of the examination-based bureaucracy and the concomitant demand to widen the basis of its recruitment to represent the needs and the talents of society more directly and completely. Although the precise reasons for his not attempting the orthodox path to advancement through the Imperial University system are hard to establish, a consideration both of Genyōsha influences and of his 'townsman's' orientation suggests that, even at the outset, he was both impatient with such a career pattern and optimistic that radical change to come would open up better opportunities for achievement. In this respect he shared with elements at both the right and left ends of the political spectrum the premise that the Restoration, though so glorious in its context, had stopped short of its full promise and needed to be completed by a further stage of 'renovation'. On the left, this becomes the completion of the bourgeois-democratic revolution as advocated by the *Kōza ha* school of Marxists and, on the right, the perfect realisation of National Polity ideals and the spread of their benign influence to bring East Asia and the world itself 'under one roof' (*hakkō ichiu*).

Nakano, however, had no dogmatic framework of this kind. He seems to have acutely sensed that rigid theorising was inadequate to the complexity of experience and that it was essential to maintain an open mind and a pragmatic or 'empirical' approach, as he usually put it, to changing situations. It was this deep-rooted pragmatism that underlay his habitual contempt for the 'intelligentsia', which he once expressed in the words: 'I am not of a nature ever to become an intellectual of the kind who plays with knowledge for the sake of knowledge'.

It also neatly fits his Yōmeigaku philosophy. As its founder Wang Yang-ming put it: 'The Sage Kings had no books'—meaning that the Sage Kings at the dawn of history, who for orthodox Confucians provided the model for all later generations, had no precedents to follow; they simply obeyed the promptings of the innate good, universal to all mankind. Later generations therefore would do better to follow their own 'inner light' rather than mechanically imitate the past. This means not merely accepting the necessity to respond to new situations in new ways, but even glorying in the opportunity to confront the infinite variety of experience and its challenges. This of course in Nakano's case is sometimes carried to a point easily described as opportunism, as in his violent *volte face* against party liberalism, his swing from anti-militarism to cooperation with the army mainstream and his changes of front on economic controls.

At the least he can be said to have kept his options open by the principle of 'metabolic' reconstruction as against doctrinaire blueprints, gathering a team of expert advisers and generally presenting a counter-example to the usual tendency to focus 'not so much on meeting specific problems as on broad moral correctives to the whole of Japanese society'.[178] Similarly he did not join in the common right wing moralistic attacks on party pork-barrel politics or Zaibatsu dollar-buying, in both of which he was to some degree involved, apparently tacitly accepting such means of financing non-bureaucratic politics as unavoidable. With a true bourgeois spirit, he publicly discounted the ideal of pure selfless service as unrealistic, for example in his last Waseda speech, and his *Outline Plan* advocated a measure of competition, together with economic guidance through incentives, in order to head off extreme controlism by bureaucracy and privileged capital, which so insisted on selflessness from humbler entrepreneurs.

It is true, however, that despite Nakano's essential 'townsman' leanings, the guise he overtly assumed was largely cast in the samurai mould, especially in his earlier and later phases. This reflects his social background on the blurred borderline between townsmen and samurai, where all the emphasis was placed on attaining samurai status and relying on samurai (or at least samurai style) leadership in struggles by the underprivileged against bureaucracy and favoured capital. As a result, the townsmen also tended to express aspirations and grievances in terms of samurai ideology rather than by anything more distinctive of their own class. This ideology may be summed up under the heading of Restorationism, the only homegrown tradition of protest, which included Confucian populism, Yōmeigaku, opposition to privilege in terms of the usurpation of imperial prerogatives and, lastly, elements of anti-foreignism.

At Waseda, however, Nakano absorbed an alternative ideology, so setting up a dialectic between radical nationalism and elements of Western-derived liberalism. The latter elements then for many years grew progressively stronger. After developing a comprehensive range of liberalistic arguments during his journalist days, he went on to engage in experimental or fringe party activity in a setting of crisis politics but later, in the stabler setting of the 1920s, largely made an adjustment with the Establishment through membership in a ruling party, the Minseitō, and vice-ministerial office. This marked his deepest point of attenuation in traditional themes and his peak of political realism. But then, when the party liberal status quo was checkmated by renewed economic and international crisis, he tried to carve out an alternative course in company with 'renovationist' elements in the Establishment, mainly army and Zaibatsu, and backed by an independent popular movement—in direct competition with his principal rivals in this endeavour, the 'new bureaucrats'.

At this stage he may be regarded as intermediate between, on the one hand, the military and the new bureaucrats, who had few ideological commitments beyond the 'national defence state', and on the other the right, whose ideological resources, though extensive, lacked much means of practical application. Subsequently, as the barriers to his success grew ever more formidable, the pattern of his career led back in reverse sequence through splinter party manoeuvres in intensified crisis politics and once more to Restorationism and *bushidō*, completing itself in a samurai form of suicide.

Ogata regards Nakano as a political failure, 'not coming up to the ankles of those in the class of Nagai [Ryūtarō] and Ōasa [leader of the IRAPS]. This judgement must at least be accepted in terms of conventional career success or in the light of Nakano's own aims, whether for himself or Japan. He did, however, make a greater impact on public life than many cabinet ministers or senior bureaucrats, in that he was Japan's most successful mass agitator. Besides, tragic though his end was, it seems to have played some part in undermining the Tōjō regime. Indeed the whole course of Nakano's last struggles vividly illustrates how far that regime fell short of being a dictatorship comparable with the nazi or Stalinist type, in that its ends had to be accomplished by a devious mixture of force and intrigue, while opposing elements remained very much alive.

It is illuminating to contrast Nakano's performance with the quite different type of success attained by Nagai, his one great rival in oratory. In their earlier Diet careers their positions almost coincided and they were closely allied. But their roots were very different— Nakano's lying in the intense tradition of Kyushu, while Nagai originated from an area never much affected by ideological or political ferment, being himself also removed from tradition by his Christian persuasion.

The parting of the ways came when Nakano left the Minseitō while Nagai remained in it; Nagai accepted the existing structure of Diet politics, while Nakano tried to bring new pressures to bear on it by mobilising less articulate sections of society. Thenceforth Nagai remained securely in the Establishment as it moved generally towards greater bureaucratisation and militarisation. He served repeatedly in bureaucratic cabinets, the IRAA and the IRAPS, more particularly as an exponent of the official Greater East Asia concept. Nakano had ample opportunities to follow the same sort of course but preferred to play a riskier game for higher stakes, evidently regarding Nagai's position as too limiting and insufficiently optimistic about the opportunities presented by the growing crisis.

To consider the reasons for the particular impact Nakano exerted, most striking perhaps was his keen sensitivity to trends, which led him to anticipate most of the major policies ultimately in fact adopted by the 'national defence state'. Such were the Greater East Asia Coprosperity Sphere, economic controls, a single political organisation, the Axis alliance, the Neutrality Pact with the Soviet Union and the Southern Advance. This was due, however, less to his influence than to his early grasp of the implications of a non-Marxist alternative to the existing internal and international order, as well as to the recognition that whoever secured the role of implementing these measures would be in a commanding position. But he never achieved this. The most that he can be regarded as achieving in the long run was preparing the public mind for measures of this sort under bureaucratic auspices–which his son regards as his real failure.

His second great talent was a remarkable skill in manipulating symbols and theory to fit a great variety of situations and programs— the key to his success as an orator. Added to these talents was the charisma arising from his particular emotional drive. He was and still is often described as 'typically Japanese', that is, typical in terms of a certain Japanese self-image which represents the essential native psyche (*Yamatogokoro* perhaps) as being, for good or evil, primarily swayed by emotion or sentiment (Nakano's passionate sincerity'), as opposed to Chinese moralism or Western rationality. A corollary, of course, is that Sinified or Westernised intelligentsia in Japan have lost something of their Japaneseness.

Nakano was no doubt typical of his milieu, but to a degree so much larger than life that he probably represented an idealised type which many of his compatriots aspired to identify with. In embodying some such plebeian image, Nakano often describes himself as uncouth or a hothead of the kind implied in his hero Saigō's saying: 'extremists are the nation's treasure'. Others often refer to his impetuousness or impulsiveness, which was certainly a factor in his long series of tactical failures.

His chronic optimism was an asset in some ways, but politically fatal when carried to such a degree of self-assurance that he was unable to work with others for long. He rejected a long series of once valued mentors such as Tōyama, Inukai, Adachi and Ishiwara and, after he had established his own political base in the Tōhōkai, his intense competitiveness or ambition made it impossible, as with all other leading figures in the right, to cooperate on equal terms in any other larger framework.

Two vivid examples of this are the abortive proposal to join the February Society and the planned merger with the Social Masses Party. His insistence on dominating these alliances is described as revealing a narrow or dictatorial quality, which was hardly compatible with his populist ideology. This should imply a basis in broad consensus rather than authoritarianism—in his own words, in Seoul days and later, a self-regulating character, at least within each sphere of activity. Apart from Nakano's own temperament, too, there was also an objective problem in the particularistic nature of Japanese social groupings, which tend to be leader-oriented. For all these reasons elitism creeps into his strategy, for example in his definition of 'social nationalism' and in the priority he gives to the nucleus in forming the IRAA. Fascism therefore came to provide a plausible model by combining the leadership principle with a kind of populism, so that Nakano tries to define totalism as combining 'democracy as end and dictatorship as means'.

Yet his sympathy for the downtrodden seems real enough, as when, in sharp contrast with the right proper, he expresses pity for humble 'proletarians accused of though crimes'.[179] He tried hard to find common ground with the labour movement, describing workers and farmers as 'Japanese among Japanese', but remained psychologically alien from labour. His rejection of socialism was fundamental—as a 'panorama' with outward appeal but lacking substance, imposing a bureaucratic uniformity which would stifle individual creativity and initiative.

In Nakano, then, formal ideology is subsidiary to his primary character drives and his essentially emotional commitment to a populist form of nationlism. As expressed by Tsukui Tatsuo, probably the most prolific authority in the renovationist right, it is very difficult to identify his 'core ideology'.[180] With unlimited eclecticism, any arguments or theories which seemed to serve the populist cause could be shaped to meet the exigencies and opportunities arising at each stage. His most thoroughly formulated program was his *Outline Plan*, drawn up in the transition between his rejection of the established parties and his later involvement with fascistic models. It probably represents the optimum practical formulation of his aspirations and he remained faithful to this basic model through the IRAA phase and during his last struggle against Tōjō and Kishi.

In accordance with his brief definition of 'social nationalism', his ideal for Japanese society could not be realised in isolation from the international scene, which for Nakano meant confronting the problem of Anglo–American domination. The Pan-Asian ideal in a modernised form seemed the most promising strategy here. In his younger days in the *Asahi* and the *Tōjō Jiron*, he seems to have genuinely sought to promote the rights of both Chinese and Koreans, as well as other oppressed peoples, but at Versailles it became starkly apparent that nationalist sentiment and interest took precedence and from then on, in increasing degrees, his interpretation of Chinese rights in particular was strictly filtered through his view of Japanese interests.

This was, of course, virtually universal in Japan but a most distinctive by-product of his earlier outlook was his invariable advocacy of friendship with the USSR as a possible ally in challenging the established international order. This attitude presents the clearest possible contrast, not only with the right, but with all influential elements in Japanese society and required a degree of courage that deserves full recognition.

The outcome of the Second World War cannot be said to have realised either Nakano's worst fears or many of his hopes. He might have welcomed the end of the colonial system in its original form but not, of course, the limited role Japan has been able to play in Asia or his country's absorption in the US-centred system of alliances. Nor has the democratisation of the Japanese political and legal system much affected the power or character of the civil bureaucracy, which has tended to dominate the single though pluralistic ruling party, as well as playing a large part in Japan's economic achievements. Much like the IRAA, perhaps, the Liberal Democratic Party has been broadly successful in manipulating the intricate interest and loyalty groups making up Japanese society, in contrast with Nakano's ideal of a dynamic mass movement as the driving force. If a vigorous populist nationalism of this type is ever to prove compatible with Japanese society, it must be some distance in the future, though his son's biographical study ends with the expression of such a hope. Placing his father in the company of Saigō, Masashige and Yoshida Shōin, foremost martyr of the Restoration, he says:

> Their spirits, through defeat, death and execution, have lived on as advocates of the will of the nation and when, in the course of history, they come to life within the nation, the nation will liberate itself and become free to tread the path to development in company with all nations.

Notes

1 Nakano Seigō 'Jiron' *Gakan* May 1935, p. 6
2 Nakano Seigō *Taikō Hideyoshi* Tokyo, 1943, p. 6
3 Nakano Seigō 'Saigō Nanshū' *Tamashii o haku* Tokyo, 1938, p. 45
4 Shibata Bunjō *Nakano Seigō kun no Omoide* Tokyo, 1968, pp. 19–20
5 Ogata Taketora *Ningen Nakano Seigō* 4th edn, Tokyo, 1952, p. 26
6 Nakano *Tamashii o haku* p. 222
7 Yasukawa Daigorō 'Nakano kun no tsuioku no ichi, ni' in Seigōkai (ed.) *Nakano Seigō wa ikite iru* Tokyo, 1954, p. 94
8 Nakano 'Kaneko Sessai O' *Tamashii o haku* p. 295
9 'Inukai Tsuyoshi' Ogata *Ningen* p. 127
10 Nakano Yasuo *Seijika Nakano Seigō* Tokyo, 1971, vol. 1, pp. 88–102.
11 Ogata *Ningen* pp. 32–35
12 'Impressions of Sun Yat-sen and Huang Hsing' Ogata *Ningen* p. 113
13 Inomata Keitarō *Nakano Seigō no Shōgai* Nagoya, 1964, p. 67
14 Nakano Seigō *Meiji Minken Shiron* Tokyo, 1913, p. 498
15 Nakano Yasuo *Seijika* vol. 1, pp. 105–6
16 ibid. p. 135
17 'Kaneko Sessai O' *Tamashii o haku* pp. 286–7
18 Nakano Yasuo *Seijika* vol. 1, p. 157
19 'Waga Sekai Seisaku no Shishin' Nakano Seigō *Kokka Kaizō Keikaku Kōryō* Tokyo, 1933, pp. 129f
20 Sugimori Kōjirō 'Nao kokumin to tomo ni iku' *Ikite iru* pp. 120f.
21 'Nyūshaji' *Tōhō Jiron* February 1917, p. 8
22 'Jiron' *Tōhō Jiron* March 1918, p. 14
23 'Jiji Hyōron' *Tōhō Jiron* January 1918, p. 35
24 'Kōkai seru Kōwa Kaigi' *Tōhō Jiron* March 1918, p. 44
25 'Ōshio Heihachirō o omou' *Tamashii o haku* pp. 91–115
26 Kokuryū Club *Kokushi Uchida Ryōhei Den* Tokyo, 1967, pp. 575–77
27 'Saigō Nanshū' *Tamashii o haku* p. 61
28 Itō Takashi *Shōwa Shoki Seijishi Kenkyū* Tokyo, 1969, pp. 394f
29 'Shin Seiji Undō no Shin Kijiku' *Tōhō Jiron* September 1920 pp. 15–23
30 Dai Nippon Teikoku Gikai Shi Kankōkai *Dai Nippon Teikoku Gikai Shi* Tokyo, 1929, vol. 12, pp. 344–5
31 ibid. vol. 12, p. 1346
32 *Kampō Gōgai* 19 February 1922, p. 283
33 *Kampō Gōgai* 21 March, 1923, p. 805
34 *Teikoku Gikai Shi* vol. 12, p. 1518
35 Washio Yoshinao *Kojima Kazuo* Tokyo, 1950, pp. 903–4
36 Nakano Yasuo *Seijika* vol. 1, p. 338
37 'Genjō Daha wa tetteiteki ni' *Tōhō Jiron* August, 1923, p. 11
38 Nakano Tatsuhiko, interview, 1970. He mentions that his father was

especially interested in the colonial ministry responsible for civil affairs in Manchuria, Korea and Taiwan
39 'Ajia no Fūunji Son Bun' *Tamashii o haku* pp. 127f.
40 Itō *Shōwa Shoki* pp. 29-31
41 'Nichiro Shinkō no Shin Kachi' *Gakan* March, 1925, p. 51
42 Asahi Shimbunsha ed. *Ogata Taketora* Tokyo, 1963, pp. 60f.
43 'Ajia no Fūunji Son Bun' *Tamashii o haku* pp. 124-6
44 'Fukanshō-shugi no sekkyokuteki Hatsudō' *Gakan* December 1924, p. 48
45 'Roshia kabure no Hyō Gyokushō [i.e. Feng Yü-hsiang] *Tamashii o haku* pp. 129-140
46 Wakatsuki Reijirō *Kofūan Kaikoroku* Tokyo, 1950, p. 322
47 Shibata *Omoide* p. 45
48 Inomata *Shōgai* p. 252
49 'Tai Shi Seisaku no Kōshin' *Tamashii o haku* pp. 146-153
50 *Yosan Iinkai Giroku* 25 January, 1929, p. 8
51 ibid. 29 January, 1929, p. 49
52 'Tōhō Jiron' *Gakan* May, 1929, p. 27
53 Sugimori Hisahide *Densetsu to Jitsuzō* Tokyo, 1967, pp. 223-6
54 Nakano Seigō *Tenkan Nihon no Dōkō* Tokyo, 1932, pp. 4-5
55 ibid. pp. 4 (introduction), 14
56 Yasukawa Daigorō 'Nakano kun no tsuioku no ichi, ni' *Ikite iru* p. 96
57 'Tōhombu ni kaeru made' *Gakan* February, 1931, pp. 24-5
58 Nakano *Tenkan Nihon no Dōkō* pp. 56-66
59 Nakano Seigō *Chintai Nihon no Kōsei* Tokyo, 1931, p. 55
60 Takamiya Tahei *Ningen Ogata Taketora* Tokyo, 1958, p. 54
61 'Mammō o ikani subeki ka?' *Tenkan Nihon* pp. 79-100
62 'Jihyō' *Gakan* November, 1934, p. 5
63 Adachi Kenzō *Jijoden* Tokyo, 1960, pp. 264-268
64 Nakano *Tenkan Nihon* pp. 16-56
65 *Kampō Gōgai* 26 August, 1932, p. 37
66 'Komai Tokuzō kun' *Tamashii o haku* p. 241
67 'Kokumin Undō e no Michi' *Tamashii o haku* p. 252
68 'Jiron' *Gakan* December 1934, p. 2
69 'Waga Sekai Seisaku no Shishin' *Kokka Kaizō Keikaku Kōryō* pp. 119-174
70 Hayashi Shigeru et al. (eds) *Niniroku Jiken Hiroku* Tokyo, 1971, vol. 2 pp. 180-191
71 'Shikkari-shiro ... Chichi' *Tamashii o haku* pp. 314-350
72 Nakano Seigō *Tenkan Nihon* pp. 72f.
73 ibid
74 Adachi *Jijoden* p. 277
75 ibid. p. 284
76 J.B Crowley *Japan's Quest for Autonomy* Princeton, 1966, p. 180
77 'Jiron' *Gakan* June 1935, p. 9
78 'Kyōryoku Seiji no Geki' *Kokka Kaizō Keikaku Kōryō* p. 213
79 Interview, 1970
80 *Kampō Gōgai* 2 December, 1934, p. 76
81 'Rōdō Undō Kōryō' *Kokka Kaizō* pp. 95-117
82 'Jihyō' *Gakan* October 1934, p. 13
83 *Kampō Gōgai* 2 December, 1934, p. 72
84 'Jiron' *Gakan* March 1935, p. 3
85 'Jiron' *Gakan* May 1935, p. 7
86 Nakano Yasuo *Seijika* vol. 1, p. 666

124 Populist nationalism in prewar Japan

87 'Jihyō' *Gakan* November 1934, p. 14
88 Mitamura Takeo *Nakano Seigō wa naze jijin shita ka?* Tokyo, 1950, p. 32
89 Mitamura Takeo 'Seigō shisezu' *Ikite iru* p. 102
90 *Kampō Gōgai* 2 December 1934, p. 77
91 'Jiron' *Gakan* July 1935, p. 8
92 Nakano *Nihon Kokumin ni gekisu* Tokyo, 1935, p. 2
93 *Kampō Gōgai* 19 February 1937, p. 140
94 Nakano Yasuo *Seijika* vol. 2, p. 335
95 'Jiron' *Tōtairiku* May 1936, p. 10
96 'Tōhōkai Daiikkai Zenkoku Taikai ni nozomite' *Tōtairiku* March 1939, p. 9
97 'Itari no Duce Mussolini' *Tamashii o haku* pp. 5, 9
98 'Jiron' *Tōtairiku* September 1940, p.3
99 'Jiron' *Tōtairiku* May 1937, p. 7
100 'Jiron' *Tōtairiku* March 1939, p. 9
101 'Dai Nippon Fudō no Dai hōshin' *Totairiku* October 1939, p. 4
102 Nakano Seigō *Sensō ni katsu Seiji* Tokyo, 1943, p. 53
103 'Jiron' *Tōtairiku* June 1936, p. 7
104 'Jiron' *Tōtairiku* June 1938, p. 5
105 Inomata *Shōgai* pp. 382–4
106 Nakano Yasuo, *Seijika*, vol. 2, pp. 118f., 259
107 Nakano Seigō *Nihon wa Shina o dō suru?* Tokyo, 1937, pp. 140–148
108 Hayashi et al. *Niniroku Jiken Hiroku* vol. 3, pp. 414–7
109 Kadota Jun *Ishiwara Kanji Shiryō: Kokubō Ronsaku shū* Tokyo, 1967, p. 210
110 'Jiron' *Gakan* April 1936, p. 5
111 *Nihon wa Shina o dō suru?* pp. 138–180
112 'Jiron' *Tōtairiku* September 1937, pp. 8f.
113 'Jiron' *Tōtairiku* October, 1937, p. 3
114 'Jiron' *Tōtairiku* January 1937, p. 5
115 Nakano Seigō *Massugu ni ike!* Tokyo, 1938, p. 109
116 Nakano Yasuo *Seijika* vol. 2, p. 336
117 'Jiron' *Tōtairiku* June 1940, p. 8
118 'Dai Nippon Fudō no Dai hōshin' *Tōtairiku* October 1939, pp. 2–12
119 'Nihon no Dōkō o kettei seyo!' *Tōtairiku* July 1939, p. 14
120 Tsukui Tatsuo *Tsukui Tatsuo shi danwa sokkiroku* Tokyo, 1974, pp. 230f.
121 'Tōhōkai wa kaku susumu' *Tōtairiku* May 1937, p. 9
122 'Jiron' *Tōtairiku* June 1937, p. 5
123 'Jiron' *Tōtairiku* July 1937, p. 4
124 *Massugu ni ike!* p. 235
125 'Jiron' *Tōtairiku* January 1939, p. 4
126 'Tōhōkai Daiikkai Zenkoku Taikai ni nozomite' *Tōtairiku* March 1939, p. 12
127 Ogata *Ningen* pp. 156–7
128 Kōan Chōsachō *Senzen ni okeru Uyoku Dantai no Jōkyō* Tokyo, 1965, vol. 3(2), p. 10
129 ibid. vol. 3(2), p. 7
130 'Jiron' *Tōtairiku* April 1939, p. 5
131 Ogata *Ningen*, p. 160
132 Yamamoto Hikosuke *Kokkashugi Dantai no Riron to Seisaku* Tokyo, 1941, p. 334
133 Kōan Chōsachō *Uyoku Dantai* vol. 3(1), p. 113–131

134 Shintō Kazuma, interview, 1970
135 Shimonaka Yasaburō (ed.) *Yokusan Kokumin Undō Shi* Tokyo, 1954, p. 15
136 Yabe Sadaji *Konoe Ayamaro* Tokyo, 1952, vol. 2, p. 99
137 Kōan Chōsachō *Uyoku Dantai* vol. 3(2), pp. 610–613
138 Shimonaka *Yokusan Kokumin Undō Shi* pp. 72–75
139 Yabe *Konoe* vol 2, p. 105
140 'Taisei Yokusan Undō no Nimmu' Satō Morio *Nakano Seigō* Tokyo, 1951, pp. 67–69
141 T. Nakamura & A. Hara 'Keizai Shin taisei' *Nihon Seiji Gakkai Nempō* 1972, pp. 96–7
142 'Jiron' *Tōtairiku* December 1940, pp. 8–9
143 'Jiron' *Tōtairiku* March 1941, p. 7
144 ibid. p. 9
145 Kōan Chōsachō *Uyoku Dantai* vol. 3(2), p. 742
146 'Tōhōkai: Kōryō, Kiyaku' *Tōtairiku* April 1941, p. 106
147 'Jiron' *Tōtairiku* October 1940, pp. 3–4
148 'Kokunan Dakai no Tai atari' *Tōtairiku* June 1941, p. 16
149 ibid. pp. 34–35
150 Satō *Nakano Seigō* p. 113
151 Kōan Chōsachō *Uyoku Dantai* vol. 3(2), p. 852
152 Nakano Seigō *Kono Issen* Tokyo, 1942, pp. 18–21
153 Nakano Seigō *Sensō ni katsu Seiji* p. 3
154 'Sōsenkyo to Tōhōkai' *Tōtairiku* April 1942, p. 8
155 Nakano, *Sensō ni katsu Seiji*, pp. 21, 39
156 Kōan Chōsachō *Uyoku Dantai* vol. 3(1), p. 132
157 'Daidō ni tsuku Tōhōkai' *Tōtairiku* June 1942, pp. 8–11
158 Kōan Chōsachō *Uyoku Dantai* vol. 3(1), pp. 138–42
159 Nakano Seigō *Kemmu Chūkō Shiron* Tokyo, 1953, p. 97
160 Nakano Yasuo *Seijika* vol. 2, p. 645
161 'Jiron' *Tōtairiku* November 1942, p. 5
162 Satō *Nakano Seigō* pp. 337–338
163 ibid. pp. 159–178
164 'Senji Saishō Ron', reproduced in Ogata *Ningen* pp. 105–10
165 Kōan Chōsachō *Uyoku Dantai* vol. 3(2), pp. 911–15
166 Interview, 1970
167 Nakano Yasuo *Seijika* vol. 2, p. 731
168 Nagata Masayoshi 'Onshi o omou' *Ikite iru* pp. 81–84
169 Okada Takeo *Konoe Ayamaro* Tokyo, 1959, p. 292
170 Yasukawa Daigorō 'Nakano kun no tsuioku no ichi, ni' *Ikite iru* p. 98
171 Mitamura Takeo *Keikoku no Kiroku* Tokyo, 1953, p. 41
172 Okada Keisuke *Kaikoroku* Tokyo, 1950, pp. 211–12
173 Matsusaka Hiromasa Den Kankōkai (ed.) *Matsusaka Hiromasa Den* Osaka, 1969, p. 225
174 Inomata *Shōgai* p. 670, quoting Hosokawa Morisada *Jōhō Tennō ni tassezu*
175 Kōan Chōsachō *Uyoku Dantai* vol. 3(1), p. 162
176 Homma Kenichirō *Kanryō Tsuihō* Tokyo, 1952, pp. 217–18
177 Inomata *Shōgai* pp. 760–61
178 E.O. Reischauer 'What went wrong?' in J.W. Morley (ed.), *Dilemmas of Growth in Prewar Japan* Princeton, 1971, p. 501
179 'Jiron' *Gakan* March 1935, p. 8
180 Tsukui Tatsuo *Danwa Sokkiroku* p. 19

Bibliography

Parliamentary and other official publications

Diet debates:
Dai Nippon Teikoku Gikai Shi Kankōkai *Dai Nippon Teikoku Gikai Shi* (Proceedings of the Japanese Imperial Diet) 18 vols, Tokyo, 1929
Kampō Gōgai (Special Issues of the Official Gazette)
Yosan Iinkai Giroku (Budget Session Minutes) 25–29 January 1929
Others:
Kōan Chōsachō *Senzen ni okeru Uyoku Dantai no Jōkyō* (Survey of rightwing Organisations in Prewar Times) 3 vols, the third in two parts; Tokyo 1965
Saikō Saibansho Jimu Sōkyoku *Shuyō Uyoku Kankei Dantai no Gaiyō* (Survey of Principal Organisations connected with the Right Wing) Tokyo, 1957
Teishin Daijin Kambō Hokenka *Shakai Undō Dantai Yōran* (Review of Organised Social Movements) Tokyo, 1933
Teishinshō Rōmuka *Teishin Rōdō Undō Shi* (History of the Communications Ministry Labour Movement) Tokyo, 1949

Periodicals

Tōhō Jiron ('The Eastern Review') February 1917 to August 1923
Gakan ('Our Views') October 1923 to April 1936
Tōtairiku (Eastern Continent) May 1936 to October 1943

Books, pamphlets, articles

Adachi Kenzō *Jijoden* (Autobiography) Tokyo, 1960
Akagi, S. 'Kokumin Saisoshiki (Imperial Rule Assistance Movement) in Nihon Seiji Gakkai *Nempō Seijigaku* ('The Annuals of the Japanese Political Science Association') Tokyo, 1972, pp. 20–70.
Arima Yoriyasu *Shichijūnen no Kaisō* (Reminiscences of Seventy Years) Tokyo, 1953
Asahi Shimbunsha (ed.) *Ogata Taketora* (Biography) Tokyo, 1963

Bibliography 127

Ashizu Uzuhiko *Dai Ajiashugi to Tōyama Mitsuru* (Great Asianism and Tōyama Mitsuru) Tokyo, 1965
Berger, G.M. *Parties out of Power in Japan 1931-1941* Princeton, 1977
Bisson, T.A. *Japan's Wartime Economy* New York, 1945
Cole, G.D.H. *The Next Ten Years in British Social and Economic Policy* London, 1929
Crowley, J.B. *Japan's Quest for Autonomy* Princeton, 1966
Duus, P. 'Nagai Ryūtarō: the Tactical Dilemmas of Reform', in Craig, A.M. and Shively, D.H. (eds) *Personality in Japanese History* Berkeley, California, 1970 pp. 399-424
—— *Party Rivalry and Political Change in Taichō Japan* Cambridge, Mass., 1968
Hasegawa Yoshiki *Tōyama Mitsuru Hyōden* (Biography) Tokyo, 1974
Hatoyama Ichirō *Kaikoroku* (Memoirs) 2nd edn, Tokyo, 1957
Hayashi Shigeru *Sensō no Jidai* (The War Period) vol. 14, Yomiuri Shimbunsha (ed.) *Jimbutsu Nihon no Rekishi* (Japanese History in Personalities) Tokyo, 1966
Hayashi Shigeru *et al. Niniroku Jiken Hiroku* (Confidential Records of the 26 February Incident) Tokyo, 1971
Homma Kenichirō *Kanryō Tsuihō* (Banish the Bureaucrats) Tokyo, 1952
Imai Seiichi and Takahashi Masae (eds) *Kokkashugi Undō* (1), *Gendaishi Shiryō* (4) (The Nationalist Movement (1), Modern History Source Materials (4)) Tokyo, 1963
Inomata Keitarō *Nakano Seigō no Higeki* (The Tragedy of Nakano Seigō) Tokyo, 1959
—— *Nakano Seigō no Shōgai* (The Life of Nakano Seigō) Nagoya, 1964
—— *Nakano Seigō to Nihon Gumbatsu* (Nakano Seigō and the Japanese Militarists) Tokyo, 1951
Itō Takashi *Shōwa Shoki Seijishi Kenkyū* (Study of the Political History of the early Showa Era) Tokyo, 1969
Jansen, M.B. *The Japanese and Sun Yat-sen* Cambridge, Mass., 1954
Kadota Jun *Ishiwara Kanji Shiryō* (Materials on Ishiwara Kanji): *Kokubō Ronsaku-shu* Tokyo, 1967
Kokuryū Club (ed.) *Kokushi Uchida Ryōhei Den* (Biography) Tokyo, 1967
Kuno Osamu and Tsurumi Shunsuke *Gendai Nihon no Shisō* (Modern Japanese Thought) Tokyo, 1956
Maejima Shōzō *Nihon Fashizumu to Gikai* (Japanese Fascism and the Diet) Kyoto, 1956
Maruyama Masao *Thought and Behaviour in Modern Japanese Politics* London, 1963
Matsusaka Hiromasa Den Kankōkai (ed.) *Matsusaka Hiromasa Den* (Biography) Osaka, 1969
Mitamura Takeo *Keikoku no Kiroku* (Record of Warnings) Tokyo, 1953
——*Nakano Seigō wa naze jijin shita ka?* (Why did Nakano Seigo End His Life?) Tokyo, 1950
Mitarai Tatsuo *Miki Bukichi Den* (Biography) Tokyo, 1958
Morley, J.W. (ed.) *Dilemmas of Growth in Prewar Japan* Princeton, 1971. Includes Najita, T. 'Nakano Seigō and the Spirit of the Meiji Restoration

in Twentieth-Century Japan', pp. 375–421
Nakamura, T. and Hara, A. 'Keizai Shintaisei' (New Economic Order) in Nihon Seiji Gakkai (ed.) *Nempō Seijigaku* ('The Annuals of the Japanese Political Science Association') Tokyo 1972, pp. 71–133
Nakano Seigō *Chintai Nihon no Kōsei* (The Rebirth of Stagnating Japan) Tokyo, 1931
—— *Kemmu Chūkō Shiron* (Historical study of the Kemmu Restoration of 1333) Tokyo, 1953
—— *Kokka Kaizō Keikaku Kōryō* (Outline Plan for National Reconstruction) Tokyo, 1933
—— *Kono Issen* (This One Battle) Tokyo, 1942
—— *Massugu ni ike!* (Go straight ahead!) Tokyo, 1938
—— *Meiji Minken Shiron* (A Study of the Popular Rights Movement in the Meiji Period) Tokyo, 1913
—— *Nihon Kokumin ni gekisu* (Manifesto to the Japanese People) Tokyo, 1935
—— *Nihon wa Shina o dō suru?* (What is Japan to do about China?) Tokyo, 1937
—— *Sensō ni katsu Seiji* (Politics to win the War) Tokyo, 1943
—— *Taikō Hideyoshi* (Lectures on Hideyoshi) Tokyo, 1943
—— *Tai Roshi Ronsakushū* Tokyo, 1926
—— *Tamashii o haku* (Expressions of the Soul) Tokyo, 1938
—— *Teikoku no Hijōji danjite kaishō-sezu* (The Empire's Emergency is far from resolved) Tokyo, 1934
—— *Tenkan Nihon no Dōkō* (Trends of Japan in Transition) Tokyo, 1932
Nakano Yasuo *Seijika Nakano Seigō* (Nakano Seigō the Statesman) 2 vols, Tokyo, 1971
Ogata Taketora *Ningen Nakano Seigō* (Nakano Seigō the Man) 4th edn, Tokyo, 1952
Okada Keisuke *Kaikoroku* (Memoirs) Tokyo, 1950
Okada Takeo *Konoe Ayamaro* (Biography) Tokyo, 1959
Satō Morio *Nakano Seigō* Tokyo, 1951
Seigōkai (ed.) *Nakano Seigō wa ikite iru* (Nakano Seigō still lives) Tokyo, 1954
Shibata Bunjō *Nakano Seigō kun no Omoide* (Recollections of Nakano Seigō) Tokyo, 1968
Shimonaka Yasaburō (ed.) *Yokusan Kokumin Undō Shi* (History of the Imperial Assistance National Movement) Tokyo, 1954
Suda Teiichi *Kazami Akira to sono Jidai* (Kazami Akira and his Age) Tokyo, 1965
Sugimori Hisahide *Densetsu to Jitsuzō* (Legend and Reality) Tokyo, 1967
Tai Ro Dankō Kisei Dōmei (League for the Breaking of Diplomatic Relations with Russia) *Tawarisshi 818-gō towa Nanibito zo?* (Who is Comrade No. 818?). No date or place of publication, but internal evidence suggests 1929
Takamiya Tahei *Ningen Ogata Taketora* (Ogata Taketora the Man) Tokyo, 1958
Tatamiya Eita *Daitōa Sensō Shimatsuki Jiketsuhen* (Review of the Greater

East Asia War: Political Suicides) Tokyo, 1966
Tsukui Tatsuo *Tsukui Tatsuo shi Danwa Sokkiroku* (Interviews) Tokyo, 1974
Wakatsuki Reijirō *Kofūan Kaikoroku* (Memoirs) Tokyo, 1950
Washio Yoshinao *Kojima Kazuo* Tokyo, 1950
Washio Yoshinao (ed.) *Kojima Kazuo Kaikoroku* (Kojima Kazuo's Memoirs) Tokyo, 1951
Yabe Sadaji *Konoe Ayamaro* (Biography) 2 vols, Tokyo, 1952
Yamamoto Hikosuke *Kokkashugi Dantai no Riron to Seisaku* (Theory and Policies of Nationalistic Organisations) Tokyo, 1941
Yamaura Kanichi *Mori Kaku* (Biography) Tokyo, 1940
Yomiuri Shimbun Seibu Honsha (ed.) *Fukuoka Hyakunen* (A Hundred Years of Fukuoka) 2 vols, Osaka, 1967

Index

Abe, Isoo, 84–5
Abe, Nobuyuki, 80, 87, 96
Adachi, Kenzō, 31–2, 35, 38, 40–1, 43, 49, 62, 69, 80, 88, 120; break with Minseitō, 44–7; Kokumin Dōmei, 54–6, 84
Agrarianists, ix, 44, 47, 61, 115
Akamatsu, Katsumaro, 53–4, 57, 61
Akao, Bin, 90, 97, 105
Amano, Tatsuo, 105, 107–110
Anglo-American influence, 28, 32, 97, 102–3, 121
Anti-Bolshevik Corps, 27, 32
Anti-Comintern Pact, 77
Araki, Sadao, 22, 31, 44, 51, 63, 65–6, 90
Arima, Yoriyasu, 38, 84, 87, 89, 92
army (or armed services), viii, 12, 56–7, 95, 101, 108, 110–11; in China, 74, 76, 79; in Manchuria, 37–9, 44–5; and Nakano, 48–9, 51, 65–8, 74, 76, 79, 81–5, 90, 101, 107, 109, 113, 117–18; political intervention, 27, 76, 79, 82, 87–9, 92, 96; and reform, ix, 54, 62, 71, 103
Asahi, 11–19 *passim*, 21–2, 44, 104, 121
Asō, Hisashi, 84
Axis, vii, 71, 77–80, 119; and Tripartite Alliance, 87, 89, 93, 106

Blood Brotherhood, 44, 47
Bose, Ras Bihari, 41, 50, 114
Britain, 18–19, 28, 74, 80
bushidō 61, 113–14, 118

Chang Ch'ün, 75

Chang Hsüeh-liang, 37–8
Chang Tso-lin, 37–8, 40
Chiang kai-shek, 37, 75
China (and Chinese), 3, 19–20, 31, 33, 36, 44–5, 50, 63, 66, 68, 74–5, 116, 121; early contacts, 9–13, 16–17; and Tanaka, 37–9; and Versailles, 21–2; war in, 76–80, 82, 85, 93
Chintai Nihon no Kōsei, 43, 60
Chōshū, 3, 6, 12–14, 27, 34
Chōya no Seijika, 11
Chūō Club, 4, 31
Clemenceau 103, 108
coalition plan (1932), 45–7, 53, 66
Cole, G.D.H., 42, 55, 60, 115
Confucianism, 1–4, 117; and Nakano, 6, 26, 37, 58, 74, 116
Constitution (1889), 3, 65, 90–1, 111; and Nakano, 14–16, 28, 33, 92
coprosperity sphere, 44, 68, 93, 110, 119
Council of State, 55, 57

Dan, Takuma, 32, 51
Denshin Denwa Mineian, 41
dictatorship, 60–1, 72, 104, 118, 120
Dōshikai, 31
Dōsōkai Zasshi, 7

East Asia League, 79
Eastern Regions Conference, 37
economic controls, bureaucratic, 73, 76, 88, 90–2, 104; Nakano on, 40, 42, 51, 55, 59–60, 73, 81, 88, 93, 97, 103, 117
elections, 88; (1917) 22, (1920) 23, (1932) 54, (1936) 80, (1937) 81,

(1942) 96–8
Electric Power Control Law, 76, 82
Emperor (institution), ix; Nakano on, 16, 55, 63–4, 94, 96, 101, 115, 117; and right wing 3, 57, 59, 64, 72, 89, 105
Emperor (reigning), 35, 94, 108
Ethiopia, 68

'family state', ix, 72, 95, 101
Far Eastern Republic, 28
Farmers' Leagues, 81, 83, 86
fascism, vii, viii, 27, 71–2, 74, 120
February Society, 81, 85, 120
Feng Yü-hsiang, 33
Foreign Policy Deliberation Committee, 19–20, 56
France, 89, 91, 103
Fukuoka, 1, 2, 36
Fukuryō Shimpō, 40

Gaikō Chōsakai *see* Foreign Policy Deliberation Committee
Gakan, 29, 41, 58, 80
General Staff, 27, 34, 107, 110
Gennankai, 7, 18
Genyōsha, 1–6, 7–8, 11, 23, 25, 40, 49, 63, 88, 116
Germany, 60, 70, 73–4, 80, 91, 97
Gondō, Seikyō, 22
Gotō, Fumio, 63
Great Japan Production Party, 84
Guadalcanal, 111

Hakata, 1, 23, 115
Hamaguchi, Osachi, 35, 40, 42–3
Hara, Kei, 12, 15, 23–4, 30
Hashimoto, Kingorō, 88–9, 92, 97
Hatoyama, Ichirō, 34, 97, 105, 108–9, 111
Hayashi, Senjūrō, 22, 81–2
Higashikuni, Naruhiko, 107, 112
Hinoshita, Tōgo, 107, 109
Hirano, Kuniomi, 2, 3, 100
Hiranuma, Kiichirō, 39, 64, 79–80, 87, 91–2, 106, 110
Hiraoka, Kōtarō, 3, 7
Hirota, Kōki, 63, 75–6, 108

Hitler, 60, 73–4, 76, 78, 80, 85, 102, 113
Homma, Kenichirō, 9, 95, 114
Honda Kumatarō, 22, 58
Huang Hsing, 9, 13

Ikeda, Seihin, 44–5, 51, 57, 82, 106
Imperial Rule Assistance Association, 72, 86–92, 96, 105, 109, 119, 120–1
Imperial Rule Assistance Political Society, 98, 105, 107, 109, 119
Imperial Way Faction, ix, 61, 87–8, 91, 106–8
Industrial Organisations Bill, 91
Information Bureau, 108–11
Inomata, Keitarō, xi, 111
Inoue, Junnosuke, 40, 42–4, 46–7
Inukai, Tsuyoshi, 8, 24, 29, 45–6, 50, 59; and Nakano, 10–13, 15, 18–19, 23, 31, 45, 54, 66, 78, 120
IRAA *see* Imperial Rule Assistance Association
IRAPS *see* Imperial Rule Assistance Political Society
Ishiwara, Kanji, 50, 58, 67, 75, 79, 82, 113, 120
Itagaki, Seishirō, 85–6, 93
Itagaki, Taisuke, 14, 103
Italy, 60, 73
Itō, Hirobumi, 3, 6, 11, 14, 65, 112
Itō, Miyoji, 36

Japanism, ix, 39, 61, 71, 73, 84, 87, 90, 97, 100, 104; *see also* right wing
'Jewish Mentality', 73, 97, 102
Jikyoku Kyōgikai, 88

Kaizō Dōmei, 22
Kakushin Club, 28–31, 58
Kakushin Shintō, 84
kakushin uyoku, vii, 88
Kanebō, 51, 86, 107
Kaneko, Sessai, 9–10, 17, 25, 45, 89
kannen uyoku, 88
Katō Kōmei, 32–3, 46
Katsura, Tarō, 11, 14–16
Kawasaki Shipbuilding Company, 27, 33

Kazami, Akira, 45, 61, 82, 87, 91;
  and Nakano, 11, 22, 29, 41, 43–4,
  46–7, 54, 57, 82, 84
Kemmu Restoration, 98, 100, 106
kempeitai (military police), 17, 67,
  100, 110–13
Kenseikai, 20, 24, 29, 31–2, 35, 40
Kido, Kōichi, 107–9
Kikakuin, 90–1, 97, 106, 108–9
Kinnō Dōshikai, 110
Kinnō Makoto-musubi, 105, 110
Kishi, Nobusuke, 92, 102–3, 110,
  120
Kita, Ikki, 14, 49, 53; and Nakano,
  22, 31, 39, 51–2, 57–60, 64–5,
  75–6
Kita, Reikichi, 39
Koizumi, Matajirō, 41
Kojima, Kazuo, 13, 16, 18, 29, 106
Kojima, Seiichi, 58
Kokka Kaizō Keikaku Kōryō, 59–
  61, 88, 91, 117, 120
Kokumin Dōmei, 54–8, 60, 68, 84,
  88
kokumin kyōdōtai, 95
Kokumin Shimbun, 12, 28
Kokumintō, 12, 20, 23–4, 28
Kokumuin *see* Council of State
Kokuryukai, 11, 22, 27, 30, 84, 92
Kokutai see National Polity
Komai, Tokuzō, 48, 66
Konoe, Atsumaro, 10
Konoe, Ayamaro, 57, 80, 90–1, 106;
  and Nakano, 76–7, 79, 82–3, 86–
  9, 101, 107–9
Korea, 3, 14, 16–17, 28, 121
Kōza ha, 116
Kuhara, Fusanosuke, 45–7
Kuomintang, 36–7, 76–80
Kusunoki, Masashige, 101, 106, 113,
  121
Kwantung Army, 37–8, 66–7
Kyushu, ix, 1–2, 4, 7, 14, 100, 118
Kyushu Electricity Association, 23,
  41
Kyūshū Nippō 40

labour movement, 54, 66, 68, 73,
120; *see also* trade unions
League of Nations, 28, 37, 48, 55, 68
liberalism, 4, 11, 13, 22–3, 48, 50,
  57, 60–1, 64, 72, 102–3, 117
Lin Ch'ang-min, 9, 13, 33
London Naval Treaty, 40, 42

Mammō Seinen Remmei, 45
Manchukuo, 9, 48, 50–1, 61, 66–7
Manchuria, 6, 9, 28, 33–4, 37–8, 67;
  Nakano in, 16–17, 28, 33, 51; *see
  also* Manchukuo
Manchurian Incident, 38–9, 44–5,
  47–8, 50, 52, 54, 65, 103
Manifesto to the Japanese People, 68,
  174
Mansen no Kagami ni utsushite, 28
Massugu ni ike! 74
Matsukata, Kōjirō, 27, 33
Matsumae, Shigeyoshi, 106–8, 112
Matsunaga, Yasuzaemon, 23, 51
Matsusaka, Hiromasa, 111
Meiji, Emperor, 13, 25, 68, 96
Meiji Minken Shiron, 13–14, 98
Mein Kampf, 103
Miki, Bukichi, 24, 31, 35–6, 46, 105
Minseitō, 31, 39–40, 43, 46–7, 53–4,
  56, 71, 80, 118
Mitamura, Takeo, xi, 67, 85, 96,
  104, 108–10, 112
Mitsubishi, 40
Mitsui, 13, 22, 26, 32, 37, 44–5, 51,
  57, 102, 106
Mitsukawa, Kametarō, 22, 29
Miura, Gorō, 13, 18, 30
Miyake, Kaho, 16
Miyake, Setsurei, 10, 16, 18, 22, 29,
  51, 58, 78, 80, 84
'Monroe Doctrine' (for Asia), 21,
  33, 50, 55, 63
Mori, Kaku, 22, 37
Mushozoku Club, 28
Mussolini, 74, 78–9, 113
Mutō, Akira, 89, 92

Nagai, Ryūtarō, 22, 24–5, 29, 31, 40,
  46, 77, 84, 89, 92, 96, 118–19
Nagata, Masayoshi, 26, 108

Index

Nagata, Tetsuzan, 44, 66
Naikaku Shingikai, 56
Najita, Tetsuo, x, 115
Nakamura, Toneo, 110–12
Nakano, Hideto, 5, 30, 53
Nakano, Katsuaki, 16, 52
Nakano, Seigō (*also* Jintarō, Kōdō, Masakata): death, x, 11–14, 118; education, 5–11; election to Diet, *see* elections; family, 5, 10; Finance Ministry Councillor, 35–6; financial backing, 23, 44, 51; Head of Kenseikai Propaganda Department, 32; horsemanship, 51–3, 113; journalism *see Asahi*, *Tōhō Jiron*; leg amputation, 35; marriage, 16; Minseitō campaign manager, 40; resignation from Diet, 85; Vice-Minister of Communications, 40–2
Nakano, Taisuke, 5, 86
Nakano, Tamiko, 16, 52, 113
Nakano, Tatsuhiko, 52–3, 112, 115
Nakano, Yasuo, xi, 52–3, 95–6, 108–9, 110, 112, 119, 121
Nakayama, Masaru, 58, 74
'national defence state', 44, 51, 65, 87, 118–19
National General Mobilisation Law, 82, 91
National Polity (*kokutai*), 88, 105, 110, 116; and Nakano, 12, 14, 65, 71–2, 84, 89, 94–5, 100–1, 109
National Spiritual Mobilisation Movement, 83
navy, 79, 106, 110–11
nazism, 71–2, 74, 83, 88, 101, 118
Nazi-Soviet Pact, 79–87
new bureaucrats, 61, 64–5, 71, 76–7, 87, 102–3, 118
'new structure', *see* Imperial Rule Assistance Association
Nichinichi, 11, 22
Nihon Kaizō Hōan Taikō, 22, 59
Nihon oyobi Nihonjin, 10, 29
Nippon Kokumintō, 39
Nōmin Remmei, *see* Farmers' Leagues

Ōasa, Tadao, 111, 118
Ogata, Taketora, xi, 6, 8, 12, 32, 44, 52, 89, 95, 98, 108, 110–11, 118
Okada, Keisuke, 56, 64, 67, 109
Ōkawa, Shūmei, 22
Ōkuma, Shigenobu, 3, 14, 31, 46, 50
'Organ Theory', 64–5, 89
Orient Youth Corps, 83, 87, 94, 103
Ōshio, Heihachirō, 4, 20
Outline Plan, *see Kokka Kaizō Keikaku Kōryō*
Ozaki, Yukio, 8, 15–16, 36

Pan-Asianism, ix, 3, 10, 114; and Nakano, 18, 32, 50, 71, 94, 96, 116, 121
'party men', 31, 39–41
Peace Preservation Law, 33
Pearl Harbour, 95, 105
Planning Board, *see* Kikakuin
Popular Rights Movement, 2, 8, 14
populism, 12, 14, 49, 57, 72, 83, 115–16, 119–20
Privy Council, viii, 36, 107, 109–10

'reconstruction', 24, 27, 31, 39, 47, 49, 56, 64–5, 75
'renovation', vii, 14, 19, 39, 47, 72, 86–7, 90, 96, 118
Restoration (Meiji, imperial), ix, 1, 4, 14, 47, 64, 103, 116, 121
Restorationism, 3, 49, 61, 64, 88, 94, 96, 100, 105, 117–18
rice riots, 20, 23
right wing, ix, 31, 64, 76, 79, 96, 106–7; and Nakano, 8, 16, 31, 39, 49, 51, 57, 65, 71, 73, 80, 81, 88–90, 92, 94–6, 104–5, 113–18, 120–1
Rōninkai, 11
Rōsōkai, 22, 29
Russia, 8, 10, 20; *see also* Soviet Union

Saigō, Takamori, 1, 3–6, 79, 99, 121; Nakano on, 14, 21, 25, 67, 96, 102–3
Saionji, Kimmochi, 11, 14, 45–6, 64

134 Populist nationalism in prewar Japan

Saitō, Makoto, 48, 50, 54, 62, 64
Saitō, Takao, 71
samurai, 1–2, 5, 14, 75, 113, 115, 117
Satō Morio, xi, 90
Satsuma, 1, 3, 15, 34
Seigōkai (Society), xi, 40, 111
Seiyūhontō, 30, 34–5, 39
Seiyūkai, 12, 14, 24, 30–1, 34–5, 39, 43, 45, 53–4, 56–7, 80
Senior Statesmen, 101, 107–10
Shakai Taishūtō, 80–6, 120
Shibata, Bunjō, 6, 36
Shichikin Hasshō, 15
Shidehara, Kijūrō, 33, 36, 39–40, 42–4, 46, 66
Shikata, Ryōji, 111–12
Shimpeitai, 95, 105
Shindō, Shintarō, 6
Shintōjuku, 89, 98
Shintō, Kazuma, 33, 58–9, 106
Shintō, Kiheita, 2, 25, 33
Shintōsha (earlier), 9, 26; (later), 89, 98
Shogunate, 2, 88–9, 93, 105, 109
Shōwa Financial Crisis, 36
Shūyūkan, 1, 2, 5–8
Siberia, 20, 23, 27, 33–4
Socialism, 27–8, 33, 41–2, 55, 81, 120
Social Masses Party, *see* Shakai Taishūtō
social nationalism, 53, 120
Sōdōmei, 61, 63
sōshi, ix, 20, 35, 39
'southern advance', 80, 86, 93–5, 106, 119
South Manchurian Railway Company, 28, 50
Soviet Union, 27–30, 32–3, 37, 49–50, 71, 77, 79, 86, 94–5, 107, 119, 121; *see also* Russia
Special Higher Police, 100, 110, 113
Special Law for Wartime Crimes, 104, 110
state socialism, ix, 53–4, 82, 115
Suetsugu, Nobumasa, 83, 88–9, 92, 96
suffrage, 24–6, 30, 32

Sugimori, Kōjirō, 18, 22, 42, 54, 58
Sun Yat-sen, 3, 9, 13, 31–2, 50

Tagore, Rabindranath, 32
Taigaikō Dōshikai, 10
Taigan no Kasai, 12
Tairo Dōshikai, 10
Tai Roshi Ronsakushū, 35
Taishō, 14, 32; Taishō Crisis, 15–16, 20, 30
Takabatake, Motoyuki, 22
Takagi, Rikurō, 22, 26
Takahashi, Korekiyo, 47, 50, 59, 63–4, 75
Takushoku University, 107
Tanabe, Tadao, 107, 109
Tanaka, Giichi, 27, 31, 34–40, 45, 50, 66
'Tanaka Memorial', 37
Teikoku no Hijōji danjite kaishōsezu, 63
Teiyū Dōshikai, 61–2
Tenkan Nihon no Dōkō, 53
tenkō, 62, 85
Terada, Inejirō, 39, 51, 90
Terauchi, Hisaichi, 76
Terauchi, Masatake, 12, 17, 19–20, 38, 56
terrorism, viii, 4, 23, 44, 74, 79, 88, 107, 110; and Nakano, 20, 49, 51, 59, 61, 90, 95, 98, 104, 108
Ting Chien-hsui, 9–10, 66
Tōa Kensetsu Kokumin Remmei, 88
Tōfūkai, 52
Tōhō Dōshikai, 98, 104–5, 109–10
Tōhō Jihō, 98
Tōhō Jiron, 8, 19–21, 25, 29, 48, 121
Tōhōkai (earlier), 21, 31; (later), 41, 58, 72, 74, 77–8, 80–9, 92–8 *passim*, 120
Tōhō Kaizō Dōmei, 58
Tōhō Seinentai *see* Orient Youth Corps
Tōjō Hideki, 79, 92, 105, 112, 114; and Nakano, ix, xi, 95–6, 101–2, 104, 106–11, 114, 118, 120
Tokonami, Takejirō, 30, 34–5, 39

Tokutomi, Sohō, 12–13, 78, 84, 96, 98, 114
Tomita Kōjirō, 46
Tōtairiku, 80, 101, 104
'totalism', 72, 81, 84, 91, 94, 120
'Tovarich 818', 34
Tōyama, Mitsuru, 2–4, 9, 41, 88, 90, 95, 114; and Nakano, 6, 7, 10, 13, 16, 18, 22–3, 25, 32, 65, 78–9, 84, 113, 120
trade unions, 32, 41, 61–3; *see also* labour movement
Tsuda, Shingo, 51, 86, 107
Tsukui, Tatsuo, 120
T'ung-meng-hui, 9
Twenty-one Demands, 20

Ugaki, Kazushige, 35, 106, 108–10
Ukita, Kazutami, 8, 11–12, 18
ultranationalists, *see* Japanists, right wing
United States, 37, 86–7, 95, 121; Nakano on, 21, 28, 38, 50, 60, 63, 76, 93–5, 108

Versailles, 21–3, 27–8, 50, 121

Waga mitaru Mansen, 17
Wakatsuki Reijirō, 34–6, 39, 44–6, 52
Wang Ching-wei, 79

Wang Yang-ming, 4, 116
Waseda, 8–11, 18, 31, 33, 40–1, 74, 102, 117
Washington Conference, 28, 33
Wilson, Woodrow, 20

Yamagata, Aritomo, 6, 11–14
Yamaji, Jōichi, 45–6, 54, 56–7
Yamashita, Kamesaburo, 44, 51
Yanagawa, Heisuke, 91, 108
Yasukawa, Daigorō, 18, 51, 108
Yasukawa, Keiichirō, 18, 22–3, 51
Yokusan Seijikai, *see* Imperial Rule Assistance Political Society
Yōmeigaku, 4–5, 17, 20–1, 25, 61, 72, 102, 116–17
Yonai, Mitsumasa, 80, 87–8
Yoshida, Shigeru, 76, 106, 109
Yoshida, Shōin, 4, 121
Yoshino, Sakuzō, 19
'young officers', 39, 44–5, 59, 66
Yugeta, Seiichi, 11–13, 16, 19, 29
Yūkōkai, 25, 80
Yūkōkyo, 26
Yūshinsha, 29

Zaibatsu, viii, 2, 4, 44, 54, 87–8, 91, 104; and Nakano, 49, 51, 64–5, 117–18
Zen, 74, 106
zentaishugi see 'totalism'